University of London Legal Series

under the auspices of
The Institute of Advanced Legal Studies

IX

THE CHARTER CONTROVERSY
IN THE CITY OF LONDON,
1660–1688,
AND ITS CONSEQUENCES

The publication of this book has been assisted by grants from the Twenty-Seven Foundation and the Queen Mary College Publications Fund

The Charter Controversy in the City of London, 1660–1688, and its Consequences

JENNIFER LEVIN

LL.M. (LOND.)

Barrister-at-law, Gray's Inn;
Lecturer in Laws,
Queen Mary College, University
of London

UNIVERSITY OF LONDON

THE ATHLONE PRESS

1969

Published by
THE ATHLONE PRESS
UNIVERSITY OF LONDON
at 2 Gower Street London WC1

Distributed by
Tiptree Book Services Ltd
Tiptree, Essex

Australia and New Zealand
Melbourne University Press

U.S.A.
Oxford University Press Inc
New York

485 13409 8

Printed in Great Britain by
WESTERN PRINTING SERVICES LTD
BRISTOL

PREFACE

THIS BOOK is an expanded version of my Ll.M. dissertation presented in 1964. As a lawyer, my main interest is the legal consequences of the attack on the charter of the City of London by Charles II in 1683. At this time, English lawyers were becoming more aware of the implications involved in ascribing legal personality to groups of persons. The struggle over the forfeiture of the charters of London, other boroughs, and other bodies such as livery companies, thus provided an opportunity for the various theories on corporate personality to be thoroughly discussed. The fact that the motives for the forfeitures were political by no means deprives the legal arguments or conclusions of their validity. A full account of the political and social implications of the forfeitures would be a very interesting though considerable task, and has yet to be done. On this point my account is necessarily brief.

I am indebted to many people for their advice and encouragement. I should particularly like to thank Professor G. W. Keeton, who was my supervisor, for having first introduced me to the subject and for his good advice and friendly encouragement. My thanks are also due to Mr D. C. Yale for his most careful reading of the manuscript and invaluable suggestions as to where it could be improved and expanded. Professor F. R. Crane has also greatly helped me and given indispensable aid towards getting the work published, for which I am very grateful. All errors and inadequacies are of course my own.

Finally I am deeply indebted to the Twenty-Seven Foundation of London University and to the Queen Mary College Publication Fund for their financial grants towards the cost of publication.

Queen Mary College   J. L.
August 1968

CONTENTS

TABLE OF CASES

CHAPTER I

Historical and Constitutional Background to the London Case

BY THE WRIT of *Quo Warranto* issued by the King's Bench against the City of London in 1682, the City were asked to show by what warrant they claimed to be a corporation. In doing this the Crown did not mean to allege that the City had never been incorporated but that, because two breaches of the City Charters had been committed, the right to those Charters was forfeited. The two alleged breaches were first, that an illegal by-law enabling the collection of tolls from persons entering the markets had been passed, and, second, that the Mayor, Common Council and Citizens had printed and circulated a seditious and malicious petition containing libels against the King and his Government.

Writs of *quo warranto* had first been issued in the reign of Edward I and it was he who used them in a systematic campaign to regulate claims by private persons to exercise all types of liberties and franchises, such as the right to hold a fair, a court or a market.[1] The theory behind Edward's campaign was that *prima facie* all such franchises belong to the King who may grant them to citizens if he wishes. Thus no citizen had the right to exercise a franchise unless he had some valid grant from the King. Those exercising franchises with no authority were ousted of that franchise; those who had authority but abused it in some way forfeited that right, and it was seized by the King. Edward's campaign was partly to deal with the abuse of franchises, but his main aim was to prevent their unjustified usurpation. The King wished to recover as many

[1] For a detailed account of Edwardian *quo warrantos* see Sutherland, *Quo Warranto Proceedings in the reign of Edward I* (1964).

franchises as possible. However, the most usual penalty in the case of abuse was not forfeiture but a fine.

Quo warrantos had been fairly commonly used since Edward's time. However, they had not been used to deprive a city of the very right to be a body corporate, to dissolve completely a validly constituted corporation. This, at any event, was the contention of the supporters of the City in 1682, and many of those who supported the King were alarmed at the idea that the ancient City of London might be dissolved.

The King, as even pro-Court observers said, was attempting to reduce the City of London to the status of a small village,[2] to place its government entirely in his own hands and to strip it of all rights and privileges. Once London had forfeited its charter, the majority of the boroughs and cities in England and Wales hastily capitulated and were induced to surrender theirs. Generally the mere threat of a *quo warranto* was sufficient to make a borough surrender. Very few attempted, even initially, to fight their cases. The 'generality of the corporations are poor decayed places, and so not able as the City of London to contest their charters'.[3] Out of over 240 boroughs and other corporations which forfeited or surrendered their charters between 1680 and October 1688, only London defended its case up to final judgement.[4] Most corporations surrendered, though the Crown actually did have to issue, rather than merely threaten, a *quo warranto* against a few others, the result being that judgement was entered by default.[5]

What were the motives of Charles II and later James II, in pursuing this course? Their aim was to control the personnel and therefore the government of the borough and city corporations over which the Crown had, in 1682, little constitutional control. Charles probably had less direct power to regulate the corporations than had any of his predecessors. Before the Civil War local

[2] *Cal.S.P.Dom.* 1683, p. 314.

[3] Roger Coke's *Detection of the Court and State*, ii, 385.

[4] London had been defeated and 'Every other corporation would be obliged to truckle'. Lord Halifax quoted by Reresby, *Memoirs*, p. 266. See Appendix A for a table of new charters granted between 1680–8.

[5] E.g., Chester, Oxford, Taunton, Worcester, Massachusetts.

government was supervised by the King through the Privy Council, but much of the power of that body over domestic matters was lost in 1641. Cromwell had tried to regulate local government by the appointment of Major Generals but this proved unpopular and was soon abandoned.[6] He also deprived some boroughs of their charters.[7] The boroughs had become very jealous of their ancient rights and privileges and resisted attempts at central control.

It was, therefore, in the borough corporations that the Whig (or Country) party could exercise most influence, which it used to the considerable embarrassment of the court. The boroughs had been the Roundheads' main strongholds during the Civil War and were traditionally Protestant, so it was from this source that Charles faced the strongest opposition when the popularity he enjoyed immediately after the Restoration began to wane.

The charters of these corporations gave them complete autonomy in their choice of officers, and they generally had the right to exclude all county officials from their precincts. In London, for instance, the Mayor and Sheriffs were elected by the Common Hall of the Freemen of the City and the Aldermen and the Common Councilmen were elected in each ward by its Freemen. The King had no direct control at all over these officers, whereas in the counties the Crown alone appointed the Lords Lieutenants, the Sheriffs (except in Middlesex), the Justices of the Peace and Militia. Having once obtained the surrender of a charter, the King would grant a new one, which, though it might contain new privileges such as a new market, would also give the Crown great control over the appointment and removal of the officers.[8] These extra privileges were considered to be 'remuneration' to induce

[6] Thompson, M. A., *Constitutional History of England, 1642–1801* (London, 1938), p. 451.

[7] E.g. Chester in 1659.

[8] See the new charter granted to Reading in 1667, It gave the Crown the right to veto the appointment of Town Clerk and Recorder, and also gave the corporation the right to hold land up to the value of £1000 per annum instead of £500 as before. See J. H. Sacret, 'The Restoration Government and Municipal Corporations', *E.H.R.*, xlv (1930), at p. 258.

the towns to surrender their charters. Many of the corporations were poor and needed all the extra privileges they could get.[9] All the new charters named the persons who should immediately take office. A clause emphasising that all officers should take the oaths of allegiance and supremacy and subscribe to the declaration prescribed by the Corporation Act 1661 was inserted. The Crown was generally given the power to remove any officer and nominate persons to fill the vacant place. The Crown also reserved the right to nominate persons to the most important positions, such as Recorder, Town Clerk or Sheriff.[10] Thus the Crown succeeded in undermining the sources of Whig power.

PARLIAMENTARY IMPORTANCE OF THE BOROUGHS

It was not merely to control local government as such that the boroughs were attacked. In fact no attempt was made to interfere with daily business except where it concerned national policy, such as the suppressing of riots and dissenters. The real importance of the boroughs lay in the fact that the majority of M.P.s were returned by them. At the elections of 1679, after the dissolution of the 'Pensioner Parliament', the composition of Parliament was as follows.

The boroughs and cities returned about 386 members, the rest of the total of 513 members coming from the Counties, Wales, the Universities and the Cinque Ports.[11] Of those returned in the 1679 elections, Shaftesbury considered that 302 members would support his cause, 158 would support the court and 36 were doubtfuls.[12] This support came from both the boroughs and the counties.[13] The Crown could deal with the Counties by replacing

---

[9] R. Coke, *Detection*, ii, 386.

[10] See the Chester charter of 1684 for example.

[11] Chamberlain, E., *Present State of England* (London, 1682), ii, 65.

[12] For Shaftesbury's list see 'Shaftesbury's Worthy Men', J. R. Jones, *Bull. Inst.H.R.*, xxx, 232. There are some omissions in this list.

[13] Of the 82 M.P.s returned for the Counties, 39 voted for the Exclusion Bill, 17 against it and 26 were absent. Shaftesbury considered that 19 of the latter were his supporters.

the Lord Lieutenants and other officials. It was the boroughs that caused the real difficulty. In many of the boroughs the franchise vested either in the freemen of the borough, a selective group often chosen by the corporation, or in the members of the corporation only, an even more select body. Many borough corporations wielded great influence over electors where the franchise depended on the payment of certain rates and taxes. Thus it was essential to control the governing body of the corporation in order to control the election of Members of Parliament. Charles's first Parliament, 1661–79, was initially sympathetic towards him, but even so he had to be moderate in his demands. It grew more and more restive and in the 1679 elections the anti-Court party obtained the large majority noted above. Control of the boroughs was vital if the Crown wanted to control Parliament. Roger North[14] admits that this was the King's aim, which he justifies by writing that it is preferable for the King to control the old boroughs rather than pack Parliament by creating new ones, which he has every right to do. It is better that the 'deluded and bribed towns' should be thus controlled. North adds, rather ingenuously, that the King could not in any case alter the right of election by renewing charters as this right depends upon prescription. However, it is obvious that to control the constitution of the body holding the franchise is to control the election of M.P.s. The new charters gave great influence to the Court, but, asks North, if the Faction had such influence they would not hesitate to use it, so why should the Court not do so?

That the Court needed to control Parliament is abundantly clear if the events of 1679–82 are studied. At this time the Whigs were well organised by Shaftesbury who succeeded in unifying a variety of different groups, mainly by concentrating on the plan to exclude the Duke of York from the throne. Concentration on this issue concealed for a time the divisions that existed between those who opposed the Court, who included religious extremists, disappointed ex-tories, those who supported the claims of Monmouth, and others. Shaftesbury also created a very efficient

[14] *Examen*, R. North. Quoted in *State Trials*, viii, 1042.

'party' organisation geared to win elections. These two factors greatly contributed to the Whig successes.[15] The revelation of the Popish Plot and Danby's secret negotiations with the French created a high water mark in Whig fortunes and they made the most of it. The Court Party was disorganised and ineffectual. The Whig House of Commons in 1679 forced the King to send the Duke of York abroad, dismiss Danby, disband much of the Army and remodel the Privy Council to admit Whig members, headed by Shaftesbury. The Habeas Corpus Amendment Act which rectified certain anomalies in the existing legislation, which had been used advantageously by the Crown, was passed. In May 1679, when the Bill to exclude the Duke of York from the Throne had passed its second reading in the Commons, Parliament was dissolved and new elections held. The new and equally Whig Parliament met in October 1680 after petitions had poured in from all over the Country for its recall. The Exclusion Bill passed the Commons but was defeated in the Lords. Stafford was impeached and beheaded for his part in the alleged Popish Plot, and the Commons passed a resolution blaming the 1666 Fire of London on the Catholics. Shaftesbury attempted to indict the Duke of York as a 'Popish recusant' and the King's mistress as a common nuisance. However, Lord Chief Justice Scroggs was ordered to break the Grand Jury before it received the depositions. At this point the differences within the Whig Party were becoming more apparent, some supporting the claims of Monmouth and others of William to the Throne. The Crown had become a little stronger and its Spanish Treaty was accepted by the Commons. Parliament was again dissolved, and the next one called in Oxford, the Court vainly hoping that tempers would be quieter there than in London. This reunified the Whigs. The Court filled Oxford with loyal regiments and the Whigs attended with armed followers; Parliament was dissolved within one week and was the last of Charles II's reign. Obviously Parliament could not be controlled merely by dissolving it, but only by remodelling the boroughs from which the Whig support

[15] See *The First Whigs*, J. R. Jones (1961).

came. The Court was encouraged by a reaction in its favour in the Country. The Whigs had behaved very violently over the Popish Plot and used every opportunity to embarrass the Court, even after it was realised that much of Oates's evidence was suspect. After the Dissolution of the Oxford Parliament, there were more addresses to the King deploring the Exclusion Bill and supporting the Dissolution than there were asking for the recall of Parliament. Shaftesbury had been accompanied to Oxford by armed followers —the same group whom he had used to intimidate moderate men in London.

The Whigs openly supported the aspirations of Monmouth, even though the true line of succession to the Throne after James went to William and Mary. The result of this was a great fear of Civil War, and an alliance between the Tories and the Court which was to crush the Whigs. Prosecutions of dissenters replaced the prosecutions of Catholics and the *Quo Warranto* was started against the City where the Whig strength was greatest.

LOCAL ADMINISTRATION

In general the King was not particularly interested in controlling the internal administration of the boroughs, even though this was frequently very corrupt. However, he was concerned when the administration of justice fell into Whig hands. London was unique in the sense that nowhere else in England were the County Sheriffs (i.e. of Middlesex), chosen by the Freemen. The Sheriffs, of course, empanelled the Juries. In all other Counties, sheriffs were selected by the Crown. But in the boroughs sheriffs were elected and juries were picked by them or by the Recorders, and thus the Whigs could rely on juries being packed with their sympathisers. In addition certain officers of the borough corporations were automatically appointed to the bench. As it was impossible by 1670 for the verdict of a jury to be attacked either by the Crown or by an individual,[16] the only way in which the Crown could ensure sympathetic juries was to control their

[16] *Bushell's Case* (1670) 1 Mod. 119.

selection. True, the judges were selected by the King and served
at the King's pleasure, but many juries brought in verdicts
directly contrary to the expressed opinions of the judge. In many
boroughs Whig officials refused to prosecute those who had
incited riots and unlawful meetings of dissenters, and hand-picked
juries refused to convict those who were indicted. North mentions
Poole and Taunton as having become 'asylums for rogues'
because justice was not administered there, and this is borne out
by entries in the State Papers. Reresby records the King lamenting
that he was the last person in the Kingdom to get justice. The
main aims of the Crown, therefore, in obtaining the surrenders
of the borough charters, were to control the officers and represen-
tative bodies of the corporations and thus, through them, the
election of M.P.s and the administration of justice and public
order.

PREVIOUS ATTEMPTS BY CHARLES II TO CONTROL THE CORPORATIONS

The *Quo Warranto* against the City of London in 1682 was not the
first time that such a measure had been used by the Crown to
deprive a corporation of its charter for abuse. However, no other
case had such great political consequences. The historic importance
of London and the fact that for three hundred years no corporation
had really defended such a *quo warranto* made the action a test case.
It was well understood at the time that if London lost then all
other corporations would have to surrender.[17] Never had corporate privileges been attacked on such a sweeping scale before. But,
although events had come to a head in 1682, Charles had been
well aware of the need to control the corporations throughout his
reign. The creation of new boroughs was the method used by the
Tudors to establish loyal corporations and a loyal House of
Commons. This was now impractical and the Stuarts created few
new Parliamentary boroughs, the last being Newark in 1673.[18]

[17] Pollexfen's argument, *State Trials*, viii, 1256.
[18] Porritt, E., *The Unreformed House of Commons* (1903), i, 382, 391–6.

Charles also tried to influence them by bribery and some election-eering (especially when Danby was his Lord Treasurer), but even though the electorate was very small, non-conformity was too well established to be removed by those means.[19] The Crown had no 'party' machinery such as that developed by Shaftesbury. From 1660 he had used two main methods to regulate the boroughs. First by means of the 1661 Corporation Act, and secondly by inducing the surrender of their charters with threats of *quo warrantos*, the latter being the most drastic and eventually the most successful.

The Corporation Act 1661[20]

The most well known provisions of this Act are those enacting that all corporation officers must henceforth take the Oaths of Allegiance and Supremacy and make a declaration denouncing the Solemn League and Covenant. They must also have partaken of Communion according to the rites of the Church of England within one year of election. By this Charles hoped to rid the corporations of dissenters. A body of Special Commissioners was appointed by the Crown to administer the Act for fifteen months until March 1663, and they exacted the Oaths and Declarations. They also had the power to remove an official from a corporation, even if he had taken all the Oaths, if they thought it was 'expedient for the public safety'. Where they had thus removed an official, they could fill the vacancy from the inhabitants of the borough. Thus for fifteen months the Crown had absolute power over the personnel of the corporations.[21] The Act also provided that no municipal charter should be forfeited because of anything done or not done before 1661. This provision was a concession gained by the Commons after hard bargaining with the ultra-Royalists in the Lords, and is significant in that it clearly indicates that it was generally thought that charters could in fact be forfeited at that time.[22]

[19] ibid.   [20] 13 Car. 2, c.1.

[21] As pointed out in *E.H.R.*, xlv, 247 (cf. n. 8).

[22] This was used by Jones J. in his judgement. *S.T.*, viii, 1265.

For fifteen months the Crown had this comprehensive control over the corporations. In fact the Court had wanted permanent control but the opposition of the borough M.P.s prevented this, which was an adequate sign, if such were needed, that Parliament would never agree to designs to subject itself to Royal power. The progress of the bill was stormy, even though the House of Commons was predominantly Royalist at that time.[23] In the Lords ultra-Royalist amendments, inspired by the Duke of York,[24] proposed that all charters would have to be renewed by 1662 on pain of forfeiture, that the Crown should have the right to appoint all Town Clerks, Recorders and Mayors, that all County Justices (who were appointed by the King) should also be justices of the boroughs within that County and, finally, that these provisions should be inserted in the charters themselves. Had these provisions been passed there would have been no need for the subsequent *quo warrantos*, as was pointed out in the debates on them in 1689–90.[25] These amendments were negatived by the Commons and the provisions set out above were passed as a compromise. The Commons did not get the right to appoint the Commissioners as they had wished but, on the other hand, the powers of those Commissioners ceased in March 1663.

At first the Act was stringently applied and many of the officers of corporations were turned out of their posts for not taking the Oaths.[26] Numerous petitions were addressed to the King from hopeful Royalists, protesting their past loyalty and asking that the Commissioners should establish them in some municipal office.[27] In Dover, a typical case, two Common Councilmen were deposed by the Commissioners in 1662 for refusing to take the Oaths, but after a year or so the Act was not enforced and open dissenters were allowed to sit.[28] The cessation

---

[23] *E.H.R.*, xlv, 249; *H. of C. Journals* 275, 291.

[24] *E.H.R.*, xlv, 250. He was a member of the Committee that proposed them and it met in his house.

[25] Merewether and Stephens, *History of the Boroughs and Municipal Corporations*, iii, 1884.   [26] For example, *Cal.S.P.Dom.* 1661–2, pp. 419, 517, 539.

[27] ibid., pp. 221, 286, 343, 628.

[28] A. F. W. Papillon, *Memoirs of Thomas Papillon*, pp. 177–8.

of the activities of the Special Commissioners made this inevitable. Also, municipal office was frequently very burdensome and it was necessary to pay a fine in order to refuse office. However, if one proved oneself incapable according to the Corporation Act both office and fine could be avoided. Such evasions were reported in Leeds, Leicester and Maidstone[29] and were probably widespread. In the case of Gloucester, the zealous activity of the Commissioners resulted in the very reverse of what the Court desired. In 1671 the Mayor petitioned for an alteration of the charter because 'it is impossible the inhabitants can supply the number it requires as almost all the wealthier citizens are those that were ejected for their disloyalty and rebellion by the Commissioners for regulating corporations'. Therefore, the Mayor said, 'we must yearly call into the Common Council men of mean degree and factious principles'.[30]

Not until 1679, when the elections to the new Parliament brought to light the Whig sympathies of the boroughs, was a determined effort again made to enforce the Act. The Privy Council appointed a committee to receive returns from certain corporations concerning their personnel. For example, in 1680, Dover was required to remove its Mayor and all those who had not complied with the Corporation Act. The Lieutenant Governor of Dover (appointed by the King, and supported by the Secretary of State, Jenkins) desired that, instead of elections, certain particular men should be placed in the vacant offices.[31]

Thus the Corporation Act did not give the Crown sufficient or permanent power over the boroughs, especially after 1663 when the Commons refused to renew the powers of the Commissioners. The only other way of controlling the boroughs was by the use of the *quo warranto*.

Surrenders and Forfeitures of Charters before 1680

(a) *Before 1660.* The use of the *quo warranto* to deprive corporations of their charters was not originated by Charles II or his

---

[29] P.C.Reg. lvii, 217.   [30] Cal.S.P.Dom. 1671, p. 4111.
[31] *Memoirs of Thomas Papillon*, pp. 179–81.

advisers. Holdsworth[32] notes that in 1628–9, 'we hear of an expedient which was to attain great notoriety in the later years of this century—*quo warranto* proceedings with a view to the remodelling of a corporation.' In the State Papers of 1628/9 there appears a note by the Attorney General that 'to accomplish the King's command touching the town of Yarmouth, they resolved to bring a *quo warranto*'.[33] The town made a faulty appearance to the writ. In 1629 a *quo warranto* was brought against Newcastle upon Tyne to question their right to be a corporation but it seems the suit was stayed at the King's orders.[34] Judgement was entered against Southampton in 1635 that all their liberties should be seized.[35] The basis of the *quo warranto* was a small defect—the neglect to certify certain customs receipts—and the reason for the action was probably to induce the town to surrender its charter. A new charter was in fact applied for in 1640. The charter of Minehead was forfeit as early as 1604.[36] The *quo warranto* was brought against Reading in 1618[37] and against Canterbury in 1624[38] but no details of these cases are available.

In the London Case, Finch and Sawyer cite many examples of *quo warrantos* from 1609–33. Some of these were for usurping the right to be incorporated and not for abusing a valid charter.[39] In all the latter cases judgement was entered by default, or a *nolle prosequi* was entered.[40] It seems clear that the *quo warranto* was being used to force corporations to submit to the Crown.

(b) *After 1660.* Charles had used the threat of *quo warranto* proceedings to forfeit charters and induce their surrender throughout his reign. None of these cases have been reported, however, and none are cited in the London Case. It has not been possible to

[32] vi, 57.   [33] *Cal.S.P.Dom.* 1628/9, p. 555.

[34] Merewether and Stephens, iii, 1662; *Cal.S.P.Dom.* 1628/9, p. 462.

[35] *Q.W. Rolls* ii Car. 1 no. 37, Davies, J. S., *History of Southampton* (London and Southampton, 1883), p. 159.

[36] Merewether and Stephens, ii, 1229.   [37] *E.H.R.*, xlv, 234.

[38] Haxted, *History of Canterbury*, ii, 642–3, cited in *E.H.R.*, xlv, 234.

[39] *Cusak* (1620), Palmer I.; *New Malton*, T.6, Jac. 11.3; *Musician's Case*, T.21 Car. r. 18; *Wygorne's Case* (1620), 2 Rolls 92.

[40] Horsham 1617; Dover 1622; Brackley 1623; Bath 1623; New Sarum 1627; Biddeford 1627; Boston 1628; Chard 1630; Bridgeport 1631; Wycomb 1633.

do a comprehensive study of all borough charters in this period, but examples collected will show that the use of the *quo warranto* against London in 1681 was no novelty. The novelty lay in the fact that only London refused to surrender and, therefore, became a test case.

From the very beginning of the reign some of the corporations had been uncertain of their legal position because of Cromwell's activities. He had deprived some of the corporations of their charters by Act of Parliament, granted new ones and had also periodically 'purged' the corporation personnel.[41] These corporations petitioned the Crown over their disputes and they were dealt with by the Privy Council or law officers, who induced many of the corporations to surrender their charters and accept new ones, by which many Royalists were restored to office. Other corporations would only surrender under the threat of a *quo warranto*. In 1661 a *quo warranto* was advised to be brought against Preston (where a 'country' party corporation was holding out against a mainly Royalist population); the charter was surrendered and a new one granted giving the King the power to nominate officers.[42] Similarly, Taunton's charter was forfeited by a *quo warranto* in 1661, on account of the town's seditious behaviour and enthusiastic support of Parliament during the Interregnum. Taunton remained without a charter for 17 years until 1677 when the usual charter giving the King power over the appointment of officers, was granted.[43] A *quo warranto* was issued against Bristol in 1660 for contempt of Royal mandates. There was considerable trouble in Bristol concerning dissenting Common Councilmen who were not removed by the Mayor despite the King's commands. Eventually Bristol surrendered and petitioned for a new charter, which was granted in 1664.[44] It seems that the Commissioners were active in prevailing upon the boroughs to surrender. In Chard the Aldermen refused to take the oaths

[41] Thompson, *Constitutional History of England*, pp. 451 ff.

[42] See *E.H.R.*, xlv, 240; *P.C.Reg.*, 1661, 416–17; *Cal.S.P.Dom.* 1661, p. 182.

[43] *E.H.R.*, xlv, 240; *P.C.Reg.*, 1661, p. 229; Savage, J., *History of Taunton*, (Taunton, 1822), p. 279.

[44] *Cal.S.P.Dom.* 1660, p. 249; 1661, p. 569; 1662, pp. 430, 490.

before the Commissioners, and the Mayor, being left alone, consented to their suggestion that he ask the King to call in the charter, 'there not being honest men enough to carry on the government'.[45]

A significant entry appears in the Calendar of State Papers of May 1661:

Warrant that in drawing up all future charters for boroughs or corporations, there be express reservation to the Crown of the first nomination of aldermen, recorders and town clerks . . . and also that there be a proviso for election to Parliament to be made by the Common Council only.[46]

This warrant was issued the day before the assembly of the new Parliament and the Court had been heavily defeated in London, but had not yet realised that the Country was predominantly Royalist. The warrant does not appear to have been acted upon in the earlier part of the reign, and in any case the enforcement of the provision concerning Parliamentary elections would have caused a storm as it was contrary to the established right that the Crown cannot alter a Parliamentary franchise set down by custom.[47]

In March 1663, when the powers of the Special Commissioners were about to expire, the Privy Council instructed the Attorney General to bring *quo warrantos* against corporations who had not renewed their charters since the Restoration[48] and examples of *quo warrantos* continue to appear. In 1663 one was issued against Berkhampsted and judgement given by default.[49] In a charter granted to Leicester in 1664/5 there is a mention of the cessation of *quo warranto* proceedings.[50] In 1666 a *quo warranto* was issued against Maidstone, and the corporation sued for pardon and a confirmation of their charter.[51] The charter of Bridport was

---

[45] *Cal.S.P.Dom.* 1661–2, p. 539.   [46] Ibid., p. 582.

[47] *E.H.R.*, xlv, 244.   [48] *P.C.Reg.*, lvi, 338.

[49] M.15 Car. 2 r.23. This is the only *quo warranto* issued in Charles II's reign that is mentioned in the London Case. Sawyer at *S.T.* viii, 1184–5, says that 'they are no corporation to this day'.

[50] *E.H.R.* xlv, 258: Stocks, H., *Records of the Borough of Leicester* (London and Cambridge, 1899–1923), iv, 501.

[51] Maidstone Corporation, *Records of Maidstone* (Maidstone, 1926), p. 153.

confirmed in 1667, with additional provisions that no writ of *quo warranto* should be issued for previous offences and that no Recorder or Town Clerk should be sworn in without the King's consent.[52] Judgement in a *quo warranto* was entered against Minehead and the Corporation was dissolved.[53] Reading surrendered their charter on being informed that a *quo warranto* was being issued against them. The grounds for this were a small maladministration of a trust fund and neglect to fill an official post.[54] A new charter gave some extra privileges, but also gave the Crown power to veto the appointment of the Steward and Town Clerk.

In the same year (1667) Clarendon was impeached, and one of the many charges against him was that:

He hath caused *quo warrantos* to be issued out against most of the Corporations of England immediately after they were confirmed by Act of Parliament.

No proof was required of this, it being said to be common knowledge.[55] However, the impeachment did not prevent the issuing of more *quo warrantos*, though they did abate a little. In 1671 Gloucester surrendered her charter under the threat of a *quo warranto* because of neglecting to fill two offices.[56] A new charter was granted in which a clause recognised for the first time that non-residents could become Aldermen (it had been the practice of the Special Commissioners to appoint non-resident aldermen; they were generally officers of State). Also Royal approval was needed for the appointment of officers.[57] In the same year the Lord Lieutenant of Ireland was directed by the King to inspect the charters, and if any town neglected to take out new ones within a certain time, he should bring *quo warrantos* against them

[52] Merewether and Stephens, ii, 1699.
[53] Merewether and Stephens, ii, 1229. It is interesting to note that Minehead continued to send members to Parliament and therefore that its privileges as a Parliamentary borough were not affected by its dissolution as a corporation.
[54] *E.H.R.*, xlv, 258. Reading Corporation Diary, no. 12, ff. 34–44.
[55] *E.H.R.*, xlv, 256, *S.T.* vi, 339, 341.   [56] *Cal.S.P.Dom.* 1671, p. 420.
[57] Merewether and Stephens, ii, 1703.

to avoid the charters.[58] In 1675 the franchises of Poole were seized into the King's hands. In 1676 the Charter of York was confirmed with the provision that no *quo warranto* should be prosecuted for any past offence. In 1680 a *quo warranto* was brought against Worcester and one was contemplated against York.[59]

It is clear that the above examples are not isolated ones and it is noted by Sacret that between 1663 and 1673 the number of new charters mentioned in the Patent Rolls far exceeds that of any other period.[60] Many of the boroughs surrendered because, whatever the legal position, it would have been too expensive to fight and too dangerous to incur the King's displeasure by so doing. But it seems certain that most were under the impression that surrender or a judgement of seizure by default on a *quo warranto*, resulted in the dissolution of the corporation, and, therefore, this was not quite the novel and unprecedented step that supporters of the City would have us believe. The differences in the situation after 1683 as compared with before 1683 were, first, that the scale of the Court's activities increased tremendously; secondly, that this policy of inducing surrenders was done openly and systematically and with the force of the London precedent behind it; thirdly, that the King had no qualms about inserting clauses in the new charters giving the Crown virtually complete control over the appointment of officers; and finally, that after 1683, the Crown did not restrict its activities to the boroughs alone, but also challenged the charters of other types of corporation, such as Livery Companies, Overseas Trading Companies, Colleges and Schools. The immediate importance of the London Case was political in that it marked the final decline of the Whigs in their last and greatest stronghold and thus enabled the Crown to pursue boldly a course which it had been more tentatively following since the Restoration.

[58] *Cal.S.P.Dom.* 1671, p. 432.   [59] *H.M.C.Ormonde*, v, 288.
[60] *E.H.R.*, xlv, 259.

CHAPTER II

Events in London Leading up to the Issue of the Writ

LONDON had supported the cause of Parliament in the Civil War and had a tradition of dissent. Even in 1661, when Charles was enjoying the wave of popularity at his Restoration, London returned four dissenters to Parliament.[1] In the same year the King complained about factious persons in London,[2] though he did not attempt to interfere with the Charter, which he confirmed in 1663, granting extra privileges.[3] He had to remind the Lord Mayor annually to enforce the provisions of the Corporation Act 1661.[4] After the activities of the Special Commissioners had ceased, this Act was laxly applied in London as elsewhere. The City was not eager to enforce strictly the taking of oaths and tests such as this, they thought, would frighten away many dissenters on whom the City's trade and prosperity depended.[5] The City was, in any case, almost bankrupt. In 1679, when anti-papist feeling was running very high, the Lords considered stricter measures against Roman Catholics in London, but dared not reach a decision lest they also frighten away the dissenters and 'shake the very trade of the City'.[6]

From about 1663 to the mid 1670s London's politics were comparatively peaceful and, although non-conformists were openly elected as sheriffs, the Lord Mayors and Aldermen were sympathetic to the Court, and many of the Common Councilmen

[1] Sharpe, R. R., *London and the Kingdom*, ii, 392.
[2] *Cal.S.P.Dom.* 1661, p. 179; 1662, pp. 594–5.
[3] See the 1662 Charter.
[4] *Cal.S.P.Dom.* 1680–1, p. 132.
[5] Kellett, *The Causes and Progress of the financial decline of the Corporation of London, 1660–1694* (Ph.D. Thesis, London, 1952).
[6] *H.M.C.Ormonde*, v, 67.

were politically uncommitted.[7] After 1677, opposition to the Court grew in London as in the rest of the Country, and London became the acknowledged leader of the Whig opposition. The 'headquarters' of the Whigs, the 'Green Ribbon' political club, was established in the City, and many old republicans gathered in Fleet Street inns. Two circumstances particularly inflamed the City. One was its bankrupt financial state, of which all attempts at remedy were defeated by the pro-Court Aldermen. The reasons for this bankruptcy were many, but at the time it was frequently attributed to the policies and extravagancies of the Court faction.[8] Charles's foreign policies had stagnated trade. He had also shut up the Exchequer in 1672 in order to pay for his Dutch War. This has often been thought to be a strong reason for London's opposition,[9] but in fact, as has been recently pointed out,[10] London did not lose much by this and there was in fact little opposition to it at that time. Secondly, the revelation of the Popish Plot in 1678 caused hysterical horror in London; many of the citizens feared that they would be massacred in their beds. This terror was exploited to the full by the Whigs. After there had been some acquittals by London juries in relation to this plot, the Whigs determined to get sheriffs of their party elected in order to control the selection of jurymen.

The Lord Mayor elected in September 1678 was Sir Robert Clayton, a Whig, and the Members of Parliament returned by the City by an overwhelming majority at the 1679 elections were four implacable Whigs, Clayton himself, Player, Pilkington and Love. They enthusiastically supported the Exclusion Bill and Pilkington even wished to impeach the Duke of York for treason. Parliament was dissolved in May in order to halt the progress of the Exclusion Bill, and the City addressed a vote of thanks to both Houses for their attempts to secure the King's safety and the Protestant religion. This had to be referred back to them because they had 'forgotten' to include the King in their thanks![11] A new Parliament

---

[7] Woodhead, *The Aldermen of London* (Ph.D. Thesis, London, 1961), p. 84.
[8] Kellett, op. cit.   [9] Norton, *Commentaries on History of London*, p. 228.
[10] Kellett, op. cit., p. 155.   [11] Sharpe, op. cit., ii, 459.

met in October 1679, the elections having gone even more against the Court, London returning the same four Members. Its immediate prorogation gave rise to a multitude of petitions for its recall from such bodies as boroughs and grand juries. London was a particularly enthusiastic and constant petitioner. Jeffreys, their Recorder, advised them against it, saying that it bordered on treason, and he was condemned by a committee of the House of Commons and forced to resign.[12] When Parliament did re-assemble in October 1680, the City thanked the King for the recall and volunteered some advice, in answer to which Charles told them to mind their own business.[13]

The year 1680 also marked the beginning of the struggle be-tween the Court and the Whigs over the elections of Sheriffs. Box and Nicholson, the Court candidates, were soundly defeated by Bethell and Cornish who gained 2000 and 2400 votes respectively as against Box's 1100 and Nicholson's 400.[14] Bethell was parti-cularly hated by the Court, having been one of the Council of State during the Interregnum and leading a life of extreme sordidness which was very different from the lavishness City Sheriffs were expected to display. Dryden wrote of him that:

> His business was by writing to persuade
> That Kings were useless and a clog to trade.[15]

Cornish did indulge in good living and was well liked by the City. However, he so incensed the Court that later, in 1685, James II extracted a particularly vicious revenge and executed him within a week of arrest, on the evidence of two pardoned traitors, before he had time to prepare a defence. The Court expressed its disgust with the elections by refraining from conferring the customary knighthood on the Sheriffs.[16]

The City continued to use every opportunity to inflame the Court. The Exclusion Bill passed through the Commons and the Lord Mayor and Aldermen accompanied Lord William Russell when he took it up to the Lords (where it was rejected). Lord

[12] ibid., p. 461.   [13] Luttrell, *A Brief Historical Relation of State Affairs*, i, 60.
[14] ibid., p. 52.   [15] *Absolom and Achitophel*, p. 583.   [16] Luttrell, op. cit., i, 56.

Stafford and other Roman Catholic Peers were impeached. Stafford was sentenced to hanging, drawing and quartering but the King commuted the sentence to beheading only. At this Bethell and Cornish presented queries to the House of Commons questioning whether the King had any power to dispense with any part of a sentence. However, the Commons were willing that Stafford should 'enjoy His Majesty's favour', and allowed the commutation mainly because they feared that by interfering they might interrupt the execution altogether.[17] The Commons passed a vote of thanks to the City for its loyalty to the King[18] and was about to repeal the 1661 Corporation Act when it was prorogued.

THE PETITION OF JANUARY 1681

The prorogation was the signal for another barrage of petitions for the sitting of Parliament, including, inevitably, one from the City of London, which was to become one of the grounds put forward by the Crown for the forfeiture of the Charter. The petitioning resulted not in Parliament's recall, but in its dissolution, and new elections were ordered for a Parliament to sit at Oxford. 'It is thought that the reason of calling the next Parliament at Oxford is, to prevent the petitioning of the City of London, and the caballing of them [The House of Commons] and the City together.'[19]

The City's petition[20] said that the Citizens of London 'were extremely surprised at the late prorogation, whereby the prosecution of public justice of the Kingdom and the making of provisions necessary for the preservation of your Majesty, and your Protestant Subjects, have received interruption'. The petition stated that Parliament had been in the process of prosecuting four of the Lords involved in the 'horrid and execrable Popish Plot' and also the Earl of Tyrone and others who were involved in an Irish Plot to massacre English Protestants. Impeachments had been voted for against Chief Justice Scroggs and other

[17] Maitland, *History of London*, ii, 468.
[18] *Journals H.C.* xv, 700-4, Jan. 1681.
[19] Luttrell, op. cit., i, 64.   [20] Text to be found in *Somer's Tracts*, viii, 144.

judges for subverting the laws of the Kingdom. All these activities had been interrupted by the prorogation and the citizens felt that the dangers of conspiracies and other subversive acts, had been increased by the activities of the King and his late Parliament. They also hoped that the petition would 'strengthen your Majesty against all Popish and pernicious counsels which any ill-affected person may presume to offer'. The petition contained much more in a similar vein, its language being described by Hallam as 'uncourtly' or even 'insolent'.[21] The Crown maintained that it was a seditious libel on the King. Certainly it was not couched in the flowery language normally used at that time when addressing the King, and it was greatly resented by him.

At the elections of February 1681 the City returned the same M.P.s who pledged that they would not vote the Crown any money until the Country was effectively secured against Popery and arbitrary power.[22] This Parliament also insisted on having its own way[23] and was dissolved in March 1681. The City thanked its Members for their services and also petitioned once again for the sitting of Parliament—which again was very ill received by the King.[24]

DECLINE OF THE WHIGS

After the dissolution of the Oxford Parliament, the Whig cause began to decline in the Country partly because it was through the Commons that the Whigs exercised their power. But in London the Whigs continued to fight and held out much longer in the face of tremendous, and eventually successful, efforts by the Court. The Court gained a few victories in August and September 1681. The King successfully prohibited a Whig banquet at which the Prince of Orange was to have been a guest.[25] An Aldermanic election resulted in the selection of Sir J. Raymond as against the Whig, Shute. In September the Court succeeded in getting a Tory, Sir J. Moore, elected as Lord Mayor. He was the senior Alderman

---

[21] *The Constitutional History of England* (London, 1872), iii, 455.
[22] Sharpe, op. cit., ii, 464.   [23] See above, p. 6.
[24] Luttrell, op. cit., i, 64.   [25] *H.M.C.Ormonde*, vi, 115.

and it would have been customary to elect him, but even so he faced opposition. However the Whigs were divided between two candidates, Gold and Shorter, and Moore obtained 300 more votes than his nearest rival, Shorter.[26]

However, the Whigs still controlled the Shrievalty, Pilkington and Shute having been elected in June despite strenuous efforts by the Court on behalf of their candidates, Box and Nicholson.[27] The election was disorderly and grave irregularities in the taking of the poll were alleged, the polling clerks being violent Whigs.[28] A series of *ignoramus* verdicts given by London Juries on bills of indictment preferred against dissenters and protestants emphasised the need for the Court to control the Shrievalty and thus the composition of juries. The bill against the protestant zealot Stephen College was rejected by a London jury in July. The case was removed to Oxford and a conviction for high treason obtained from a jury of eminent Tory gentlemen of that county. In October, Rouse, a servant of the Whig, Sir Thomas Player, was accused of high treason for alleging the King to be a Papist. The bill was declared *ignoramus* by the jury. London juries would seldom find for the King and Reresby quotes the King as saying he was the last man to have law and justice in the whole Nation. The climax came with the bill brought against Shaftesbury for high treason. Despite a paper alleged to have been found in Shaftesbury's room by the Secretary of State, Jenkins, which contained plans for the formation of an association to defend the Protestant Religion and to exclude the Duke of York from the Throne, the jury returned the bill marked *ignoramus*. Bonfires were lit all over London to celebrate the denial of the bill (November 1681).

The Court had considered various ways to secure a favourable verdict in the Case. In the Ormonde Papers, Lord Longford

[26] Sharpe, op. cit., ii, 476; Luttrell, op. cit., i, 128–9. The figures were: Moore, 1831 votes; Shorter, 1560 votes; Gold, 1523 votes. The fact that the Whigs could not agree on a single candidate is indicative of their increasing lack of unity.

[27] Luttrell, op. cit., i, 102. The figures were: Pilkington, 3144; Shute, 2244; Box, 1266; Nicholson, 84.

[28] Reresby, *Memoirs*, p. 234.

writes that the Court were considering whether the Bailiff of Westminster could legally return a jury to hear the case, and cases against the 'rest of his gang', on a special commission of Oyer and Terminer. This depended on the charters granted to the Abbot of Westminster and the City. Judges were to deliberate on the question.[29] However no more is heard of it. After the acquittal, it was obvious to the Crown that the only way to achieve permanent control over the City was to remodel its Charter, and to do this the Charter had first either to be surrendered or forfeited. On 26 November 1681 Secretary Jenkins wrote that so great was the insolence and riot on Shaftesbury's acquittal that the King resolved to see how far a *quo warranto* could be maintained against the City.[30] An undated entry in the State Papers considered to have been written in November 1681 sets out a number of queries concerning the grounds for a *quo warranto* to be submitted to King's Counsel.[31] These references are the earliest that have been found to a *quo warranto* against the City of London.[32] On 21 December the writ was delivered to the City Sheriffs and this considerably alarmed the City and the Whigs. On the same day they were even more alarmed, and the Court considerably encouraged, by the results of the elections to the Common Council, 'out of which number in Sir Robert Clayton's Ward eight of the late *ignoramus* jury, who were then of the Common Council, are excluded and two men of them are left out in other wards'.[33] The Court hoped that the government of the City would be in the future 'quiet and loyal' but if by this they hoped that the question of the Charter would be speedily solved they were mistaken. On 18 January 1682, the Common Council were formally notified of the service of the Writ and they appointed a committee to defend the Charter. On this Secretary Jenkins wrote that 'our friends' carried everything they

---

[29] *H.M.C.Ormonde*, vi, Oct. 1681, p. 211.   [30] ibid., Nov. 1681, p. 238.

[31] See below, p. 24; *Cal.S.P.Dom*. 1681, p. 682.

[32] Woodhead, op. cit., mentions a reference in *H.M.C.Ormonde*, v, 288, for March 1680/1 but this refers to the City of York, not London.

[33] *H.M.C.Ormonde*, vi, 278; see also *Cal.S.P.Dom*. 1680-1, p. 638; Luttrell, op. cit., i, 153.

had intended by leaving the defence of the City to the 'other party,' there being 'a probability it will go against the City'.[34]

However another year was to elapse before the hearing of the case started (in February 1683) and judgement was not given until June 1683. The Court may at first have been confident of winning but they were by no means certain of it. There are numerous references in the State Papers of 1682–3 showing the King's anxiety for the conclusion of the Case,[35] and he always hoped that the City would agree to surrender the Charter on his terms rather than fight to the end and incur its forfeiture. The Court had many doubts before it finally settled the two causes of forfeiture on which to base its case. An entry in the State Papers[36] shows that the election and activities of the Sheriffs were contemplated as grounds for the *quo warranto*. Another proposed ground was the alleged illegal selling of offices by the sheriffs, and the exaction of numerous tolls. Also in this entry are set out the conditions under which the King would regrant the Charter if the City surrendered. They are very similar to those eventually offered after the judgement. Obviously the Court hoped that the City would surrender. The City showed very little inclination to appease the Court in any way throughout (though after judgement was given the Common Council refused to surrender by only a small majority, after a lengthy debate). In June 1682 came the climax to the battle over the election of the Sheriffs.

THE STRUGGLE OVER THE SHRIEVALTY, 1682

The right of electing sheriffs had always been a subject of dispute. Until 1638 the Mayor had always exercised the right of nominating and electing one of the sheriffs. This right was then not exercised for three years and when, in 1641, the Mayor again

[34] *Cal.S.P.Dom.* 1682, p. 34; Sharpe, op. cit., ii, 477. The Committee consisted of Lawrence, Clayton, Ward, Flavell, Ashurst, Hawkins, Hammond, Morris and Godfrey.

[35] *Cal.S.P.Dom.* 1682, p. 142; 1683, pp. 227, 296, 300, 367.

[36] *Cal.S.P.Dom.* 1681, p. 682.

claimed the right, the Commons declared he had forfeited it by misuse. From 1641–63 the right was either not exercised, or, when claimed denied by the citizens (who however always elected the Mayor's choice). From 1663–74 the right of the Mayor passed unchallenged but in 1674 the custom of the Mayor nominating a sheriff by drinking to him at a banquet was first recorded. The right was challenged but no decision was reached and the mayor's right remained unchallenged from 1675–9. In the years 1680 and 1681, the Common Hall elected both sheriffs, the Whigs Cornish and Bethell in 1680 and Pilkington and Shute in 1681. The Mayors of those years were also Whigs, of course, and therefore raised no objection. The King was determined to control this important office and was unwilling to await the conclusion of the *quo warranto*. The Court Party had difficulty in finding a candidate, because of the possible retribution of Parliament, but eventually Dudley North was prevailed upon. The Lord Mayor, the Tory Moore, was requested by the King to drink to North at his banquet, and when the Common Hall was held on 24 June the Mayor requested that North be confirmed as sheriff and another elected. This was greeted with cries of 'no confirmation' and a demand for a poll. The Whigs Papillon and Dubois were elected, defeating North and Box (the other Tory candidate), the Sheriffs conducting the poll ignoring the Lord Mayor's order to adjourn it after seven o'clock. The poll was adjourned until 5 July and then again adjourned by the Lord Mayor, but the Common Hall refused to comply and Papillon and Dubois were again declared elected[37] by the Sheriffs. There were further adjournments, riots and confusions, and eventually the King intervened and ordered new elections, the previous ones being pronounced irregular, and declaring North to be one of the Sheriffs. What happened at this poll is confused. The official records shows a poll as between Box, Dubois and Papillon, which Box won. However, Luttrell and the writers of certain pamphlets declare that a second poll was held between all four contestants

[37] The figures were: North, 1557, Papillon, 2754; Box, 1609; Dubois, 2709. Luttrell, op. cit., ii, 203.

which the Whigs won.[38] There followed numerous petitions asking that Papillon and Dubois be declared elected, to which the Mayor avoided making any answer. Then Box paid a fine rather than serve, the Mayor announced yet further elections, and there were further petitions and angry scenes. It was customary for those Livery Companies whose members were elected Sheriffs to elect them Masters of the Company. The Weavers and Mercers reinforced the results of the previous polls by electing Dubois and Papillon respectively.

After further dissensions, both sides presenting petitions to have their candidates declared elected, a Common Hall was called to elect a sheriff to accompany North. Rich was nominated as Tory candidate and in the din that followed this announcement a poll was said to be called for. The Mayor then hastily declared Rich to be elected and went home. Whereupon the Sheriffs held a poll, declared Papillon and Dubois elected and dissolved the Common Hall speedily before the Mayor arrived back on the scene. The Mayor and Aldermen reported the proceedings to the King. Pilkington and Shute were told that they would have to appear before the King's Bench for riotous behaviour, and on 28 September North and Rich were at last sworn in as Sheriffs despite the protests of the Whigs. Thus, as Luttrell pointed out, the Mayor had in effect nominated both Sheriffs. The Court Party was victorious, and their victory was reinforced by the election of a Tory Lord Mayor, Pritchard, who narrowly defeated Cornish, though there were allegations of irregularity at the poll by both sides.

The results of the elections, although undoubtedly obtained by illegal means, marked the turning point in Tory fortunes in the City. The proceedings had been managed by Leoline Jenkins, who completely dominated Moore.[39] It is significant that even the Whig pamphleteers considered Moore to be weak rather than

[38] The Lord Mayor's figures: Box, 1244, against Papillon and Dubois, 60. Luttrell gives the following figures for the second poll: North, 107; Box, 173; Papillon, 2482; Dubois, 2481, against confirmation, 2414. Luttrell, op. cit., ii, 206: Guildhall Tracts A no. 18.

[39] North, *Examen*, pp. 600–1.

wicked, misled by the Court.[40] The Duke of York had openly taken part in the elections[41] and the King had delayed his departure to Newmarket until the battle was won.[42] All the forces of the Court had been used to defeat the Whigs and it is indicative of their (the Whigs) strength in London that the struggle was so lengthy and in the end only won by force. The army had been called out to subdue the angry Whigs and 300 people who had opposed North and Rich were imprisoned for one month. On the face of it the Tories had triumphed. The dissenters were violently prosecuted and many were excommunicated by the Ecclesiastical Courts in order to incapacitate them in the forthcoming Common Council elections and thus produce a Common Council willing to surrender the Charter.[43] The King and the Duke of York were magnificently entertained at the Guildhall. Juries were now as amenable to Tory interests as they had previously been to those of the Whigs, and they awarded the Duke of York the fantastic sum of £50,000 damages against Pilkington for *scandalum magnatum*, fined him and Shute for riot during the elections and convicted Patience Ward of perjury during the Shaftesbury trial. There was also the revelation of the Rye House Plot and the flight of Shaftesbury and other leading Whigs to Holland, which left the Whigs in disarray.

However, the Common Council elected in December despite a rigid enforcement of the Corporation Act, was not prepared to surrender the Charter to the King, and his victory over the Shrievalty was only temporary and would have to be engineered afresh each year. It was obvious that complete and permanent control over the City could only be achieved by forfeiting the Charter and thus the hearing of the *quo warranto* began in the King's Bench in February 1683.

That the King would be victorious was made very probable by the changes he then made in the judiciary. In April, Dolben, who disliked the *quo warranto* against the City, received his *quietus*, and

---

[40] 'A Modest Enquiry Concerning the Election of Sheriffs'. Anon. (1682).
[41] R. Coke, *Detection*, quoted in *S.T.*, viii, 1082.
[42] *H.M.C.Ormonde*, vi, 440.   [43] Luttrell, op. cit., ii, 242.

his place in the King's Bench was taken by Wythens, who gave judgement in the London Case even though he had heard only one argument (the first being held on 7 February, before he was appointed). Saunders, who had drawn up the pleadings for the Crown, was nevertheless appointed Lord Chief Justice of the King's Bench in the place of Pemberton, who was removed to the Common Pleas.[44] North comments ingenuously on this, 'The King, observing him to be of a free disposition, loyal . . . thought of him to be Chief Justice of the King's Bench at that nice time. . . . So great a weight was then at stake as could not be trusted to men of doubtful principles or such as anything might tempt to desert them'.[45] When the Case was first argued, Luttrell notes that 'many are of the opinion it will go against the City'.[46] Later, after noting the strict prosecution of the dissenters in London, he remarks that most men now seemed to be Tories.[47]

The events in the City inspired many polemical pamphlets, both supporting and abhorring the King's action. Apart from that of L'Estrange,[48] they add little to the arguments advanced in the case itself. Those supporting the City see the case as the climax of a Papist plot to destroy the Protestant Religion and the Constitution and deliver the Nation to the French King. One Pamphleteer even suggested that the King might now issue a *quo warranto* against the House of Commons, a younger body than the City, and one which had also acted in an unmannerly fashion of late towards the King.[49] The pamphlets summarised the legal arguments and listed the great losses that would result to the Citizens if London were reduced to the status of a village.

---

[44] Burnet, *History of My Own Time*, ii, 343; Foss, E., *The Judges of England* (London, 1848–64), vii, 163.

[45] *Lives of the Norths*, i, 296.   [46] Luttrell, op. cit., ii, 249.

[47] ibid., p. 252.   [48] 'Lawyer Outlaw'd' (1683).

[49] 'A Modest Enquiry Concerning the Election of Sheriffs' etc. (1682).

CHAPTER III

The Arguments of the Crown and the City

THE main points of argument in the *quo warranto* proceedings against the City of London were as follows. First, and most important from both the legal and the constitutional point of view, is the dispute as to whether the King could demand the forfeiture of the right to be a corporation, and thus dissolve the corporation. Second, could a *quo warranto* for the forfeiture of the Charter of the City be brought against the corporation as a body in view of the fact that the information denied its corporate personality? The City maintained that such an information could only be brought against the individuals comprising the corporation in their separate capacities. Third, were the alleged illegal acts of the Common Council, which were the grounds for the forfeiture, in fact the acts of the Corporation? If they were not, they could not result in the Charter's seizure. Fourth, was it possible for a corporation to commit a crime? Fifth, assuming these illegal acts were the acts of the Corporation, were they sufficient grounds for forfeiture? Sixth, was London, by virtue of certain statutory provisions, in a specially protected position as compared to other corporations?

The case was opened for the Crown by Mr Solicitor Finch, whose relatively brief argument seems to be a prelude to the more lengthy and thorough examination of the issues by the Attorney-General, Sawyer. Treby, the Recorder of London, and Pollexfen appeared for the City, and had the advantage of arguing last. (All the references to the case in the footnotes are to the Cobbett edition of *State Trials* (1810), Volume viii.)

I. IS A CORPORATION CAPABLE OF BEING FORFEITED BY THE CROWN?

The Crown maintained that the franchises can only be granted by the King, a grant which is always accompanied by a trust. Abuser of this trust incurs forfeiture of the franchise.[1] The right to act as a corporation is a franchise (or liberty), and not a mere capacity as the City alleged,[2] and, therefore, subject to the same laws as other franchises. Treby says there is but one case[3] wherein a corporation was called a liberty, and that 'one swallow does not make a Spring', but in fact there are many others.[4] To call a corporation a mere capacity to sue and be sued, to take and to grant, is as ridiculous as it would be to say 'that a man is a mere capacity to walk with two feet.'[5] The Crown puts forward many authorities to show that the abuser of a franchise or liberty results in its forfeiture. However there seems to be a tacit difference of opinion between Finch and Sawyer as to the precise nature of the judgement for which they are asking and consequently whether there are any direct authorities for it. Finch says:

But, my Lord, there are many cases of like nature, and that even in the case of the City of London too, as I shall show you by and by. Now tho' these are not judgements in *Quo Warrantos*, to out a corporation of a franchise of being a corporation, yet it shows, that these things were forfeitures of all the franchises of a corporation; for a seizure is never but where there is matter for forfeiture apon record . . . But in the case of 9 E.1 then it does appear Judgement was given by the Parliament, that the liberty should be forfeited, not that it should be seized into the King's hands only . . . Indeed I do not find any judgement in a *Quo Warranto* of a corporation being forfeited.[6]

Finch seems to be making a distinction between the seizure of a corporation's liberties into the King's hands and their forfeiture. He is asking for a judgement of forfeiture of the being of the

---

[1] Many authorities are cited for this (which is not denied by the City), i.e. 18 Ed. 2 (*St. de Quo Warranto*); 2 Inst. 223; *Shrewsbury Case* 9 Co. 50; *Bagg's Case* (1616) 11 Co. 98. See *State Trials*, viii, 1088, 1171.

[2] See below, p. 34.   [3] *Helmsley* (1620) Co. Ent. 527; Palmer 9.

[4] *S.T.*, viii, 1103.   [5] Sawyer, p. 1159.   [6] *S.T.*, viii, 1090.

corporation, for which he acknowledges there is no direct precedent, and which, from the opinion he gave to the City after the case, would seem to be more drastic than mere seizure, as it would entirely dissolve the Corporation. He also says that seizure of all the liberties of a corporation would in effect forfeit its existence as the corporation would be 'nothing at all'. Sawyer, however, quotes the judgements of the old cases as being the same as the judgement for which he is now asking[7] and that is seizure of liberties. Forfeiture is the ground on which seizure and ouster are both based, and seizure, whilst not amounting to ouster, nevertheless dissolves the corporation. It would appear that Sawyer considers that seizure would suspend the operation of the corporation, so that the King takes over its government, and dissolves the corporation in so far as it enables the King to grant a new charter (which could not be done so long as the old one was in existence). He says that it is not the design of the King to reduce the City to the status of a country village but merely to place a *custos* over it, as did Edward I, Edward III and Richard II. Those seizures did not destroy the ancient customs and privileges of the City. This difference between Counsel is again shown in the opinions of the counsel given to the City after the case.[8]

Sawyer cites many old cases, which, he says, show clearly that a corporation can be and has been forfeited. In the case of *Sandwich*,[9] an offence committed by the Mayor and officials of the Corporation resulted in the entire Corporation losing its liberty ('amittat libertatem suam'). Sandwich had lost its franchise before[10] when the Mayor had neglected to put down a riot. The King in Parliament, acting, Sawyer insists, in a judicial and not a legislative capacity, ordered that the liberties should be seized as forfeited. The Town was thereupon delivered up to the government of the

---

[7] ibid., p. 1179; *Sandwich*, P.9 E.1, r. 35; *Cambridge*, 8 R.2. no. 11; 4 Inst. 228; *Winchester*, 33 E.1, *Plac. Parl.* 277. *Memoranda de Parliamento*, no. 456; *Ipswich*, M.18. E.3, r. 161; *Norwich*, *Close Rolls* 7 John m. 24; *Oxford*, 32 H.3, m. 13; *Evesham*, 26 H.3, m. 8; *Southampton*, 18 E.1 *Rot. Parl.*, i, 58; *New Malton*, T.6 Jac. 1 r. 3; *New Radnor*, M.20 Jac. 1, r. 17.

[8] See below, pp. 51 ff.   [9] P.9 E.1, r. 35; *Placit. Abbrev.* 273.

[10] (1275) 3. E.1.

Common Law. The City of Cambridge[11] lost its corporate right owing to a riot. The Court ordered the Town to answer concerning their privileges, a plea was entered by the Town and their liberties were seized, the record showing that:

Nostre Seigneur le Roy de assent des Prelates & Seigneurs en cest Parliament fist seiser la dit franchises en sa maine comme forfeit pur la ditz causes.

In his account of this case Coke inserts in the margin, 'Nota, by Act of Parlt.', giving the reference.

This leads Treby to allege that, although this was a seizure of the corporate right, it was not a judicial but a legislative act.[12] Sawyer replies that Treby is misled by Coke's account of the case which is 'lamentably defaced' by the marginal note,[13] which miscites the record of the case as 8 R.2.11. The real record is 5 R.11, 45–66, and the judgement was undoubtedly judicial, it being quite usual in those days for the King and Parliament to sit as a judicial court. In the case of *Ipswich*,[14] the judgement upon a forfeiture was:

quod custodia eiusdem Villae seisiatur in manus Regis.

Sawyer cites further cases[15] as examples and there are many more of that era that he could have cited. There are numerous instances of the seizure of the liberties of London itself. For example, in 1265, London having sided with the Barons against Henry III, their liberties were seized, a *custos* appointed to govern them, and the liberties only restored on the payment of a fine.[16] Similarly, they were deprived of their liberties by Richard II and a *custos* put over them.[17] All these cases, says the Crown, show that a corporation is capable of being forfeited. More recently, *quo warrantos* have been issued 'in Mr. Attorney Palmer's time' for the franchise of being a corporation, but they all resulted in judgement by default or in submission to the King, says Finch.

[11] 8 R.2, no. 11; 4 Inst. 228; 5 R.2, 45–60, *Rot. Parl.*, iii, 106.

[12] *S.T.*, viii, 1112–13. Treby does not deny that an Act of Parliament can dissolve a corporation.

[13] ibid., pp. 1180–1. 4 Inst. 228.   [14] M.18 E.3, r. 161.

[15] See footnote 7 above.   [16] 49 H.3.   [17] 16 R.2 *Pat. Rolls* m.36 (1392).

Sawyer also quotes these cases.[18] It would be strange, Finch considers, if a corporation could be ousted for ever of their franchise for neglecting to appear, and yet 'when all the Contempts and Oppositions imaginable are found upon record, that this should not be a forfeiture . . .'[19]

Another point made by the Crown, though they acknowledge that it is not strictly relevant to this case, is that a corporation can be surrendered. It is acknowledged by both sides that things may be forfeited which are not surrenderable but nevertheless each side argues this point, the City maintaining that corporations cannot be surrendered[20] and the Crown maintaining that they can.[21]

The City alleges that, by its very nature a corporation is immortal and cannot be dissolved save by Act of Parliament or death of all its members. Sawyer answers that a corporation is composed of human beings who have been given the right to act as a corporate entity. It can only act through its members. It is ridiculous to maintain that anything made by and composed of natural persons can be immortal. What Coke and the other authorities meant when using this term was that where any gift is made to a person, such as the mayor in the corporate name, it does not determine on the death of that person. A corporation is immortal only in the sense that it subsists as long as there is someone capable of holding that right. Thus there is no essential difference between the right to act as a corporation and the right to any other franchise. *James Bagg's Case*[22] is direct authority for the Crown, says Sawyer. In this case it was held that if a person commits an act contrary to his sworn duty as a freeman of a corporation, he shall lose the right to be a freeman. What one person in a corporation can do, they all can do together and thus all the members can lose their right to act as a corporation.

---

[18] *New Malton*, T.6 Jac., r. 3; *New Radnor*, M.20 Jac. 1, r. 17; *Berkhampsted*, M.15 Car. 2, r. 23; *Helmsley*, Co. Ent. 527; *Ferrers* (Virginia Co.) 2 Rolls 455. See *S.T.*, viii, 1150.

[19] *S.T.*, viii, 1090.

[20] *Dean and Chapter of Norwich's Case* (1590) 3 Co. 73, Dyer 273 b; *Hayward* v. *Fulcher* (1628) 3 Co. 73, Jones 166.

[21] *Archbishop Bruerton* v. *Dublin* (1569) Dyer 282.   [22] (1616) 11 Co. 98.

The disastrous consequences of not being able to forfeit corporations for wrongdoings were emphasised by the Crown:

How many Oppressions and Offences would be daily committed, if every Corporation were a franchise and jurisdiction independent upon the Crown?[23]

To punish the individuals alone would be inadequate 'where the power of offending and misgoverning should still remain'. The granting of large franchises has always been feared because they tend 'to the overthrowing of the Common Law'.[24] If the members of a corporation can,

vote raising of men against their Prince; and should give authority to levy money for that purpose; [commit] Murders, Felonies, and Oppressions of their fellow subjects,[25]

and yet not be forfeited, then they function quite outside the reach of the Common Law and 'it would be unsafe, either for the King or any of his subjects to live in or near a Corporation'.

The City denied that the Court had the power to forfeit a corporation. True, franchises and liberties were forfeitable if abused, but the right to be a corporation was not a franchise, but a mere capacity to sue and be sued, to take and grant. Coke refers to a corporation as a capacity and so does Brook.[26] In only one case is a corporation referred to as a franchise.[27] Franchises are estates and inheritances, capable of being granted and conveyed from one to another, but the right to be a body politic cannot be conveyed and cannot be included in the general term, 'franchises'.[28] By its very nature a corporation cannot be forfeited, for it can

[23] Finch, *S.T.*, viii, 1090.
[24] ibid., p. 1091; Commons Petition 21 E.3, *Rot. Parl.* 17.
[25] Sawyer, *S.T.*, viii, 1149.
[26] Treby, *S.T.*, viii, 1101 ff.; 1 Inst. 250; Brook's Abridgement, Part 1 fol. 182 b.
[27] *Helmsley*, Co. Ent. p. 527.
[28] Pollexfen, *S.T.*, viii, 1244; he also mentions the Statute of Gloucester, 1278, 6 E.1, whereby all who claimed franchises were to come and justify them before the Justices in Eyre on pain of forfeiture. There is no record of a corporation having to come and justify its claim to be a body politic. Coke, 2 Inst. 278, says this Statute applies to such franchises as waifs, felons' goods etc., but he does not mention the right to be a body corporate as a franchise in this context.

never die. The City produces many authorities to show that a corporation is: 'Invisible, immortal and rests only in intendment and consideration of law.' It

cannot commit Treason or Felony, be Outlawed, Excommunicate, hath no Soul, cannot appear in Person, cannot do Fealty, cannot be imprisoned, not Subject to Imbecility or Death.[29]

Treby quotes Grotius as saying 'cities are immortal'.[30]

The only powers that a corporation has are those given it by the law. If it does any act that the law does not authorise, then that act is not the act of the corporation but only of the individual members, and only they are answerable for it.[31] 'The Being of a Body Politic is but a Capacity, and in resemblance to a Natural Body, and no more forfeitable than a natural Body.' A man cannot forfeit his denizen status, and it has also been held by the Court and the House of Lords that a peer cannot surrender or in any way dispose of his peerage.[32] The privileges of being a denizen or a peer are granted by the King, as is the right to be incorporate, yet they cannot be forfeited by the King. The City alleges that a corporation can only be dissolved by an Act of Parliament or where all its members are dead. Even so there is the case, mentioned by Coke, of Old Sarum, which, though decayed, remained a borough.[33] In Roll's Abridgement, only death is considered as dissolving a corporation, not abuser.[34] Coke mentions a minor Welsh custom which, having grown unreasonable, could be extinguished only by Act of Parliament. Should not the extinguishment of a great corporation require similar treatment?[35]

The Crown have no authority for their claims, says the City. If this power of forfeiture existed, one would imagine that it would

[29] Pollexfen, p. 1260; *Sutton's Hospital* (1612) 10 Co. 23a.

[30] *De Jure Belli & Pacis* L2, c9 s3. Madox, *Firma Burgi*, points out at p. 49 that Treby does not complete the quotation, which reads, 'Dixit Isocrates, et post eum Julianus Imperator, civitates esse immortales, *id est esse posse*'.

[31] Pollexfen, p. 1260.

[32] *Earl of Oxford's Case*, Jones, p. 97; Petition of Ld Purbeck to Lords, Treby, p. 1108.

[33] Treby, p. 1107.   [34] Pt. 1 fol. 514, 'Corporation'; Treby, p. 1105.

[35] 2 Inst. 664; Treby, p. 1108.

have been used before, but not even Henry VIII, when dissolving the monasteries, thought of doing it by a *quo warranto*. Why did he go to such trouble, asks Treby,[36] to seek out abuses in the abbeys, to appoint men as heads of these corporations who were instructed to surrender them, and to confirm the surrenders by Statutes, if the slightest abuse would have justified a forfeiture on a *quo warranto*? Those old seizures of towns put forward as precedents by the Crown[37] were not seizures of the corporations themselves, but merely of particular franchises and liberties which had been abused, such as the mayoralty.[38] The King never intended to destroy the corporations but merely to keep the peace. In the case of London, for instance, the Courts and customs of the City continued as before, as is shown in the London Records.[39] Had the corporations themselves been forfeited, new privileges would have had to be granted, and yet, once the fine was paid, the King *confirmed* the old privileges. Many of these corporations (*e.g.* Bristol and London) claim to be so by prescription to this day, which they could not so claim had they been dissolved and new ones subsequently set up by charter. Pollexfen stresses that all the seizures quoted by the Crown are 300 years old and 'no such thing was ever done since' those troubled and disordered times. Such precedents should not be followed unless afterwards considered and approved, and no law-book has ever taken any notice of them. It has never entered men's heads that a corporation might be forfeit. If it had why was it necessary to pass numerous Statutes[40] regulating penalties for abusing rights? Why were the corporations not forfeited? There are numerous examples of *quo warrantos* being brought to forfeit individual franchises, but it was not suggested in them that the entire corporation should be forfeit.[41]

Concerning the surrender of corporations, Treby relies on the

---

[36] *S.T.*, viii, 1107.   [37] Those cited in note 7 above; also *Bristol, London.*
[38] Treby, pp. 1113 ff.; Pollexfen, pp. 1248 ff.
[39] E.g. The Court of Hustings and of Aldermen continued to function—*Liber Albus* fol. 50, 51, 125; Pollexfen, p. 1252.
[40] 15 Hen. 6, c. 6; 19 Hen 7, c. 7; 12 Hen. 7, c. 6; etc. See below, pp. 44 and 66 for Sawyer's answer to this.
[41] *Heddy* v. *Welhouse* (1597) *Moore* 474.

cases of *Hayward* v. *Fulcher*, and the *Dean and Chapter of Norwich's Case*, where it was held that a Dean and Chapter cannot surrender their corporation.[42]

Pollexfen refers to Sawyer's contention that the King does not wish to destroy the City corporation, despite the form of the pleadings, but merely to seize it and govern it. This is impossible, says Pollexfen, the effect of the judgement can only be to dissolve the corporation entirely. A judgement on a *quo warranto* is one of right and therefore conclusive and unalterable on both the King and the City. 'We are not now in the irregular days of the records mentioned.'[43] In any case, even if the judgement could be one of seizure and not forfeiture, this could not be carried out, for in whom could the corporation subsist? A corporation is not transferable, and the King cannot possibly hold it. In *R.* v. *Staverton*,[44] a *quo warranto* was brought for keeping a Court Baron. A judgement of ouster, not seizure, was given as the King cannot hold a Court Baron, for it is a liberty incident to a Manor and not derived from the Crown.

But what can he [the King] do when he has seized the corporation? Can he himself be the Mayor, Commonalty and Citizens of the City of London? or can he put in any one to be such corporation? It is not a thing manuable 'tis not a Thing seizable, nor ever was seized.[45]

Either the corporation remains where it is, or it is completely dissolved.[46]

As to the evils which the Crown says will result if a corporation is not forfeitable, the City holds these do not exist, but that far greater evils would result if the Crown's contentions were correct. To the charge that a corporation could raise rebellion and yet go unpunished if it could not be forfeited, Pollexfen replies[47] that corporations are under the same law as individuals and if the members of a corporation do an unlawful act, either the

---

[42] *Hayward* v. *Fulcher* (1628) Palmer 491; *Dean and Chapter of Norwich* (1590) 3 Coke 73. The question of the legality of the surrender is not relevant to the London Case, but is important in relation to the subsequent surrenders. See further Ch. 7.   [43] Pollexfen, *S.T.*, viii, 1259.   [44] Yelverton, 191.
[45] Treby, *S.T.*, viii, 1114.   [46] Pollexfen, *S.T.*, viii, 1251, 1259.   [47] ibid., p. 1242.

corporation can incur penalties or the Members are personally liable. In a case of 21E.4[48] it was said by Pigot that a mayor and commonalty cannot commit treason, but if all the members of that commonalty do so each is severally liable. Any other law would result in great injustice as well as being ridiculous as a small minority of wrong doers and every little peccadillo could forfeit the rights and privileges of the innocent majority and all the debts and rights dependent on the corporation would be destroyed. In London particularly, many evil consequences would arise from a judgement of forfeiture.[49] All the corporation lands would revert to the donors and all customs claimed by prescription would be destroyed. Many of these, Pollexfen declares, are annexed to this Charter and cannot be transferred to any new Charter that the King might grant for a new corporation, for a new corporation cannot be in succession or privity with the old. This is why the preservation of the old Charters was so insisted upon in the *Dean and Chapter of Norwich's Case*[50] and *Hayward* v. *Fulcher*.[51] Judgement for the Crown would render every corporation in the country unsafe and: 'who will trust a corporation, if its duration and existence be so fickle and infirm, that every abuser or misuser shall forfeit it?'[52] What is the purpose of the many Acts of Parliament, including Magna Carta, made in previous times to confirm the liberties of London if when 'they lay but 6d. apon a joynt of meat they are gone, and there is not a month in the year but they forfeit their being?'[53]

2. AGAINST WHOM SHOULD THE INFORMATION BE BROUGHT?

The City:[54] To bring an action against the City in its corporate name, alleging that it is not in fact a body politic, is illogical. By directing the writ to the City, the Crown admits that it is a

[48] Y.B. 21 E.4, fol. 13.   [49] Pollexfen, *S.T.*, viii, 1257.
[50] (1590) 3 Coke 73; 2 Anderson 120.   [51] (1628) Palmer 491; Jones 166.
[52] Pollexfen, *S.T.*, viii, 1258.   [53] Treby, ibid., p. 1144.
[54] Treby, ibid., p. 1116; Pollexfen, ibid., p. 1214.

corporation.[55] In the case of *Cusak and Others*[56] an action was brought against individuals for usurping to be a guild corporation. Hale also says that where a *quo warranto* is brought against a corporation for usurper, it must be brought against individuals because judgement must be given that they shall be ousted of the corporation.[57] In the case of the Town of *Helmsley*[58] the action was brought against the Mayor, Helden, and others for usurping the corporation. There are other similar examples.[59] Pollexfen claims that the judgement must prevent the corporation from continuing to usurp, and also fine it for having usurped in the past, for usurpers must always be fined. But how can the Corporation, which is extinguished by the judgement, also pay the fine?

There are, the City admits, many cases[60] where a *quo warranto* was brought against a corporation for claiming to be one. These cases can be distinguished on the following grounds. First, they were brought for claiming other liberties besides that of being a corporation and therefore as regards those liberties the actions were well brought. None of them was exactly like the present *quo warranto* for the right to be a corporation alone. Second, none of these cases came to final judgement; either a *nolle prosequi* was entered, or a surrender was recorded. Only the case of *New Malton*[61] proceeded to judgement. Here an action was brought against the Bailiffs and Burgesses of New Malton for claiming certain liberties, including that of being a body politic. Judgement was given that their liberties be seized and they be fined. However Pollexfen has a number of objections to this case as a precedent. First, judgement was *sub silentio*, no authorities being quoted for it,

[55] It should be noted that the form of the writ of *quo warranto* is the same, whether usurper or abuser of a corporation is alleged.

[56] (1620) Palmer 1.

[57] Hale, *Commonplace Book* 168 pl. 7 (not printed, but quoted in Anon., *Law of Corporations*, 1702).

[58] Co. Ent. 527; Palmer 9.

[59] *Maidenhead Case* (1260) Palmer 80, 81; *Bermudas Co.*, T.6 Jac. 1, r. 3.

[60] None of them are reported e.g. *Reading*, M.3 & 4 Eliz. r. 4; *Horsham*, Hil, 14 Jac. r. 37; *Dover*, H.19 Jac. r. 26; *Bath*, H.20 Jac. 1; *Biddeford*, M.2 Car. 1, r. 36; etc.

[61] T. Jac. 1, r. 3.

and it has never been mentioned in any law book. Second, how could the corporation pay the fine when it ceased to exist? Third the case constitutes but a single example, and the borough was' small and totally in the power of the local lord. Last, the case is not quite the same as the present, as in fact the borough had never been incorporated.

The Crown: Sawyer[62] argues that the action can be brought either in the corporate name, or against individual names followed by some general description. A general name is used merely to identify those against whom the action is brought, and does not indicate that the King acknowledges that the body referred to by the general name is incorporated. If the King wishes to allege a body to be incorporated it must be specially pleaded and cannot be inferred from the name by which the body is sued,

so that *Mayor, Citizens and Commonalty of London* being a general name, sufficiently describing the persons against whom the suit is brought, may be used in the King's suits without any manner of conclusion to the King.

There are numerous examples of *quo warrantos* being brought in the same form as this to question the corporation.[63] In fact, by using this argument, says Sawyer, the City admits that the liberty of being a body politic may be seized, provided the action is brought against the particular persons, and the cases before cited show that in fact it can. Those cases cited by Treby[64] prove that corporations are franchises and can be questioned and seized by a *quo warranto*. The suits are brought against some persons by name and the rest of the corporation by general words, such as 'et alios liberos homines', and the judgement binds the whole corporation. The case of *Cusak* was against certain persons by name, 'cum diversis aliis Civibus Civitat "Dublin"' and judgement was

---

[62] *S.T.*, viii, 1150 ff., and p. 1184.

[63] *Denbigh*, H.27 Eliz. r. 15; Co. Ent. 537 *Chard*, B.R.5 Car., r. 28; *Canterbury*, H. Car. 1, r. 25; *New Radnor*, M.20 Jac. 1 r. 17; *New Malton*, T.6 Jac. 1, r. 3; *Berkhampsted*, M.15 Car. 2, r. 23.

[64] *Cusak* (1620), Palmer 1; *Virginia Co.* (1624) 2 Rolls 455; *Helmsley*, Co. Ent. 527; *Bermudas Co.*, T.6 Jac. 1, r. 3.

against both those men and the corporation. Sawyer also argues that where the King proceeds for the forfeiture of a corporation for breach of its charter, the right of incorporation does not determine until judgement of seizure, and until then the corporation remains *de facto* and is capable of being sued. The judgement is final, however, and Sawyer says that it does not admit a fine, as Pollexfen alleged. In all the old cases when fines were paid, they were not imposed by the Court as part of the judicial proceedings. They were imposed by the King as a condition of restoration of the franchises.

The city was concerned to put forward every possible objection to the Crown's case. Even assuming that a corporation could be forfeited, which they denied, they argued that the two causes of forfeiture did not have this effect. The publishing of the petition and the passing of the by-law to collect tolls were acts of the Common Council. Assuming the petition to be seditious and the by-law to be illegal, which they again denied, the City maintained that they could not result in the forfeiture of the Corporation as the acts of the Common Council had not been shown to, and did not bind the Corporation. Also, it was suggested that a corporation was incapable, by its very nature, of committing a crime or doing anything illegal.

3. DO THE ACTS OF THE COMMON COUNCIL BIND THE CORPORATION?

Pollexfen[65] first objects that nowhere in the pleadings are the powers of the common council set forth, and in the City's replication it is only stated that the Common Council has had the power time out of mind to make by-laws and ordinances for the regulation of the markets. Thus if they do have this power, its exercise will obviously not forfeit the Corporation, but if they do not, how can an unauthorised act of the Common Council forfeit the existence of the entire Corporation? The Crown does not set forth on the record that the Common Council has the power to

[65] *S.T.*, viii, 1236.

bind the City, and, as the powers of the Common Councils vary so much, the Court cannot be expected to take notice of that of the City. Treby[66] says that the Common Council is a body of but 250 men, the City comprising 50,000 men, who have the power only to advise the City, not to bind it.[67] Its powers depend upon custom and a custom 'shall never be construed to enable a man to do a Wrong', and therefore they cannot act in such a way to deprive the City of its Charter. If the Common Council does an act beyond its powers, that act is void. The King 'gave them a power to make reasonable By-laws, and so he does every Corporation. And the same Law that gave them the Power, limits that power, and says if they go beyond that power, it is a nullity'. How can a void act of the Common Council forfeit the whole Corporation? The members responsible for the act will have to answer for it, but not the Corporation. No charter has ever given the Common Council the power to surrender or forfeit the Corporation, so where should they get such a power, asks Pollexfen. He adds a further point[68] that both of the alleged offences were done in the names of the 'Mayor, Aldermen, and Citizens in Common Council assembled', and not in the name of the Corporation. Therefore the act was not done under the Common Seal, and the Corporation cannot be held responsible for those acts.[69]

Sawyer counters this argument effectively.[70] A corporation can only act through its members, and there are authorities showing that a corporation is liable for the wrongs of those members. A clear case is that of *Lincoln*,[71] where two Burgesses wrongfully took a toll. It was argued that their acts did not bind the corporation but held that the act of the two officers was in fact the act of the corporation.[72] If it is true, as the City alleges, that only those

---

[66] ibid., 1141 ff.   [67] *Eastwick's Case* 2 Rolls 456.
[68] At p. 1239.   [69] 12 Hen. 7, 25, 26; 9 E.4, 39.
[70] *S.T.*, viii, 1185 ff.   [71] 48 Ed. 3. Y.B. fol. 17 b.
[72] There are many other like cases which Sawyer does not mention in this context. See Sandwich, *Placit. Abbrev.* 273, where it was held that any act done by the Mayor in matters affecting the community, was an act of the Community itself and Sandwich accordingly forfeited its liberties on account of the Mayor's trespass.

acts done under seal are properly the acts of the corporation, then no Mayor or Sheriff can legally act, as they are not chosen under seal, neither are any of the by-laws valid as corporate acts as they were not passed under seal. In the case of *Cambridge*[73] two Burgesses were authorised by the Common Council to appear on the City's behalf and this was held good even though not done under seal.

Sawyer then demolishes the contention that the City is specially protected from the consequences of the illegal acts of its officers by virtue of Statute 1 E.3. (Finch discussed this Statute in relation to the claim that the City's Charter could not be forfeit for future misdeeds, and he concluded that it could not be held good even in the narrower sense that the City should not forfeit its Charter on account of the misdeeds of its officers.) According to the *Liber Albus*[74] (this Statute does not appear in the Patent or Parliamentary Rolls) Statute 1 E.3 provides 'quod libertas civitatium Londinarium capiatur in manum Domini Regis pro alique personalia transgressioni, vel judicio personali alicuius ministri eiusdem civitatis'. In fact neither Treby nor Pollexfen (who of course argued after Sawyer) stresses this Statute (or Charter). Pollexfen uses it in another context and Treby, although he considers that the two illegal acts did come within its provisions,[75] nevertheless denies that he needs to rely on this Statute to support his case. The reluctance of the City to use it may be explained by Sawyer's effective reduction of its operation.

The wording of this Statute, he says, shows that previously the Corporation had been forfeited for the personal misdeeds of its officers. This Statute relieved that state of affairs but did not extend this relief to miscarriages of government by officers. Neither did it prevent excessive fines being inflicted on the officers or protect the City if the offence was committed a second time. Therefore Statute 28 E.3, c.10[76] was passed. By this Act, defaults

[73] 5 R.2, 45–60 *Rot. Parl.*, iii, 106.

[74] ii, 147.

[75] At *S.T.*, viii, 1143.

[76] (1354) 2 *Statutes at Large*, p. 99. This is extensively discussed in a pamphlet by L'Estrange, 'Lawyer Outlaw'd' (1683).

of the Mayor, Sheriffs and Aldermen would be punished in the first instance by a fine of 1000 marks, for the second default, 2000 marks, and for the third default the franchise and liberty of the City should be taken into the King's hands. The defaults were to be investigated by juries drawn from areas outside London. This Statute also applied only to personal transgressions of officers and if the members committed such 'outrageous acts . . . as breach of their duty and good government', then these settled penalties did not apply. This act was amended by 1 H.4, c.15[77] which provided that

the penalty aforesaid, as well as the 1000 marks, and of the 2000 marks, and of the seizure of the franchise comprised in the said Statute, shall not be limited to a certainty, but that the penalties in this case by the advice and discretion of the Justices thereto assigned, as other cities and boroughs . . .

The effect of this Statute is to make the penalties discretionary and does not affect the City's liability to have its Charter forfeited for bad government. L'Estrange points out that in view of the discretion given to the Judges by this Statute, if the crimes of the officers were very grave, the judges could immediately proceed to forfeit the Charter. Thus, this Statute, though it was passed at the request of the Citizens and thought by them to be of benefit to themselves, 'in crime of State, where the Crown and Monarchy are concerned, 'tis no less an advantage to the King'.[78] Sawyer ends his argument on this point by giving a lengthy list of authorities showing that a franchise may be seized on account of the activities of the Common Council.[79]

These two Statutes, 28 E.3 and 1 H.4, seem to be very clear authority in favour of the Crown's allegations, not only that the Corporation is liable for the acts of its officers, whether assembled

---

[77] (1399) 2 *Statutes at Large*, p. 398.

[78] L'Estrange, 'Lawyer Outlaw'd'.

[79] See p. 1192; for example: *Pat. Rolls* 4 E.2, Part II m. 22 (1321) which is an appointment of Robert de Kendale to the Office of Mayor of London which had been taken into the King's hands by judgement of the justices in Eyre at the Tower.

in Common Council or not, but also in support of their contention that the liberty of the corporation can be seized if abused. It is not therefore surprising that Treby and Pollexfen give them little attention.

4. CAN A CORPORATION COMMIT A CRIME?

This question is closely allied to the previous one as to whether a corporation can commit an illegal act so as to forfeit the charter. The discussion provides an interesting illustration of a problem in corporate law which was eventually settled only in the mid-nineteenth century. In the pleadings the Crown alleged that the City 'unlawfully, maliciously and seditiously' published a petition censoring the King for proroguing Parliament. Thus the Crown alleges that a corporation can commit an indictable crime, that of criminal libel, and is capable of having malice aforethought. Treby denies that a corporation can commit a crime,[80] and his basic reason is the same as that for declaring that a corporation is a mere capacity and cannot be forfeited. A corporation is a mere *ens rationis*, it has no body, soul or mind. Accordingly it cannot have the evil or malicious intention which it is necessary to establish in proving the commission of a crime.

A corporation is but a name, an *ens rationis*, a Thing, that cannot see or be seen, and indeed is no substance, nor can do or suffer Wrong, nor anything where a corporal Appearance is requisite.[81]

How could a corporation be punished if it were indicted for a crime such as treason, asks Treby. 'What? Must they hang up the Common Seal?' This does not mean that they can raise insurrection with impunity, as those persons who, ostensibly acting as the corporation 'go out of their corporate business' and commit treason are severally liable. Also, if the corporation were liable for treason in that capacity, then the individuals who actually committed the offence will not be liable in their personal capacities as a man cannot be twice liable for the same crime. Thus, as the

[80] Sawyer's answers to the last point apply equally to this point on whether a corporation can commit a crime.   [81] Treby, *S.T.*, viii, 1138.

corporation cannot sustain the punishment laid down for treason —imprisonment or death—the Crown's claim amounts to a dispensation to commit crime with impunity. Treby lists authorities in none of which, he says, is it stated that a corporation can be proceeded against for a crime.[82]

5. ARE THE TWO OFFENCES SUFFICIENT GROUNDS FOR FORFEITURE?

The two offences alleged by the Crown were that the City had passed an unlawful by-law permitting the collection of tolls in the markets, and that they had published a malicious and seditious petition libelling the King and his Government.

(a) *The Tolls:* The City's Rejoinder stated that they were seized of the markets and had a power to raise reasonable tolls for their upkeep, and that therefore the by-law was valid. The Crown said that they were not seized of the markets and had no responsibility for their maintenance. The markets were intended to be free, and in any case they could not have a power to levy reasonable tolls as this was too uncertain to be a custom. This dispute is not really of any general interest. The greater part of the case is conducted on the assumption that the passing of the by-law was illegal, and on balance it would seem that the Crown is correct in contending that it was illegal. The Crown is plainly of the opinion that the slightest infringement of a charter can result in its seizure, but nevertheless both Sawyer and Finch attempt to make this by-law appear a gross extortion of money for private profit and therefore a heinous oppression of the people and derogation of the Royal Prerogative.[83] It is plain that the by-law was passed by the Common Council with genuine belief in its validity and in order to obtain the means to repair some of the damage created by the Fire, so that it is ridiculous for the Crown to try to make it appear that this offence was anything more than a technical excuse for forfeiture.

[82] e.g. Stamford, *Pleas of Crown*; Coke, *4th inst.*; Hale, *Pleas of Crown*.
[83] Sawyer, *S.T.*, viii, 1195 ff., Finch, p. 1097.

The City answers that the offence might justify the forfeiture of the markets but how can it affect the being of the City? Can the existence of the City be said to be incident to its markets? There are many cases where by-laws were declared illegal, but the corporation was not thereby forfeited,[84] including a case against the City for Water Bailliage dues. The Crown declares that this offence concerns the highest point of trust vested in a corporation, that is, its law-making powers, and this incident to the very existence of the corporation. Those cases cited by Treby can be distinguished on a number of grounds. They were suits between the corporation and a private party and the Court was not called upon to consider how far the by-law entrenched upon the Royal Prerogative; also there is a difference between by-laws regulating the internal affairs of a corporation and those for the levying of money.

(b) *The Petition:*[85] The Crown alleged that the Petition was a malicious libel on the King and the question as to whether or not a corporation can commit a malicious crime has already been dealt with. The City maintained that they had no evil intent when presenting the Petition but were motivated entirely by a desire to protect the public and allay its fears, it being lawful to petition the King. They also allege that the contents of the Petition were true; public justice was interrupted by the prorogation of Parliament, although this does not necessarily impute an evil motive to the King. The Crown replies that the Petition was *prima facie* libellous and neither good intent nor truth is a defence to *scandalum magnatum.*[86] They do not deny that petitioning is lawful, but say that lawful acts can become unlawful if done with evil intent. The Crown lays great stress on the malice displayed by the City in the composition and publication of the Petition.

THE JUDGEMENT

The arguments of counsel concluded on 30 April 1683 and judgement was not given until the following 12 June. It was expected

---

[84] *Maidenhead* (1620) Palmer 77; Treby, *S.T.*, viii, 1128–30; Pollexfen, p. 1231.
[85] See above, p. 20 for details of its contents.   [86] Finch, *S.T.*, viii, 1097.

that judgement would go for the King[87] in view of the pre-
parations that had been made by him. The brilliance of the
Attorney General's argument was commented upon, and what
was especially stressed by the Court supporters was Pollexfen's
failure to answer the point that if charters could not be forfeited for abuser there would 'be so many commonwealths by
themselves, independent on the Crown and in defiance of it'.[88]
However, confident though the King might have been that the
case would go in his favour, he was very anxious that judgement
should be given and impatient at the delay. He considered that
'a few days being sufficient for examining the precedents', judgement could soon be given.[89] He also made the revealing comment
that, having heard from all sides of the strength of the Attorney
General's arguments and the weakness of Pollexfen's, 'there will
be no indecency in it'. The ill health of the Lord Chief Justice
(Saunders) caused anxiety and the King desired to avoid all
'accidents'. (Indeed, an accident was only narrowly averted, for
Saunders died the day after judgement was given.) It is plain from
the State Papers that the Court officials were doing their utmost to
expedite the whole affair.[90] It was the King who suggested that
Jones should give the judgement instead of the sick Saunders, and
this was done.

Judgement[91] was given by Jones, Raymond and Withens
indicating their agreement. Saunders, being ill, was not present,
but was said to agree. It was held that a corporation might be
seized, and that this appeared from Statute 28 E.3, c.10 (concerning penalties where the Mayor of London fails to enforce
order, discussed at pp. 43–4) and also 12 Car 2, c.11 (Act of Indem-
nity, 1660) whereby corporations are pardoned of all past crimes and

[87] Luttrell, *A Brief Historical Relation of State Affairs*, i, 249. See above, pp. 27–8.

[88] See *Cal.S.P.Dom.* 1683, pp. 222–3; letter from Francis Gwyn to the Earl of
Conway. See also comments of like nature by L'Estrange.

[89] *Cal.S.P.Dom.* 1683, p. 227: letter from Sunderland to Jenkins.

[90] Ibid. and p. 296. Jenkins was required to consult with 'the Lords who usually
meet at your[Jenkins'] lodgings and consider well what can be done'. Other court
advisers would have preferred the less drastic course of surrender.

[91] *S.T.*, viii, 1265 ff.

offences, and 13 Car 2, c.1 (Corporation Act, 1661). The taking of the toll by the illegal by-law and the libellous Petition were a good cause for forfeiture. The Acts of the Common Council did bind the Corporation and the Information was well founded. Accordingly the franchise of the City of London should be seized into the King's hands.

Jones apologises for not making his judgement into a formal argument because of lack of time. He says little beyond enumeration of the points of the decision set out above. He does however make the point that, if the contrary had been held, then 'little republics' would spring up all over the Kingdom, which would not be conducive to good government. He gave no opinion as to the capacity of a corporation to *surrender* its franchises.

Naturally the brevity of the judgement gave rise to adverse comment, as did the fact that one of the Judges, Withens, had only heard one of the arguments. Burnet says the judgement 'was given without the solemnity that was usual upon great occasions'.[92] In his advice to the Common Council after the case on whether or not they should surrender, Treby considered that the fact that the judgement was so speedily and briefly given meant that the Judges had not really intended that the effect of their judgement would be to dissolve the Corporation. Had they intended this they would have taken more time and consulted with all their colleagues, as was customary in novel cases far less important than this one. In fact it is clear that the unseemly speed was due to the King's impatience and not to the nature of the legal points involved. It was also rumoured that Saunders had been too ill to give any opinion at all on the case, and when the other Judges asked him for his decision, he told them not to bother him for he had lost his memory.[93]

[92] *History*, ii, 346; North (*Examen*) disagrees with him of course but on this he is particularly unconvincing. See *S.T.*, viii, 1059.

[93] R. Coke's *Detection*, ii, 313. Note by Sir John Hawkes, *S.T.*, viii, 1356. Maitland, *History of London*, p. 479.

CHAPTER IV

The Effect of the Judgement in London

SURRENDER OR FORFEITURE?

THE JUDGEMENT was that 'the liberty, privilege and franchise aforesaid, to be of themselves one body of corporate and politic, in deed, fact, and name, by the name of Mayor, Commonalty and Citizens of the City of London . . . to be taken and seized into the hands of the Lord the King'. The effect of this gave rise to further dispute. The Attorney General asked that the judgement be not entered until the King's pleasure be known and the City therefore took the opportunity, after much debate, to ask for pardon. They acknowledged with sorrow their past misgovernment of the City, thanked the King for not entering the judgement, and promised their future loyalty. The reply to this was given by the Lord-Keeper, North, who told them that the apology would have been more acceptable if it had been made sooner, but that the King was prepared to show reasonable favour to the City as he knew that there were many loyal citizens amongst the factious. The King would not forfeit the Charter if the City would submit to the following conditions: first, no Lord Mayor, Sheriff, Recorder, Common Sergeant or Coroner should be admitted to office in the City unless the King approved of the appointment; second, if the King twice disapproved of their choice of Lord Mayor, he should have the power to appoint one, and the same should apply to the appointment of Sheriffs; third, the Court of Aldermen should have the power to disapprove appointments, and they might also decide that a person elected as an alderman was unfit, in which case the election should be held again; if they again disapproved, the Court of Aldermen itself would fill the vacancy; fourth, Justices of the Peace were to be of the King's Commission and their appointment left to the Attorney and Solicitor Generals. If the City would agree to these conditions, the King would pardon the prosecution and confirm its Charter, in a manner consistent with the conditions.[1]

Should the City submit or fight to the end? On 20 June the City accepted the King's terms after long debate and a draft deed of surrender was drawn up. However, even at this point the opposition was not crushed. The draft surrender and other queries were sent to four counsel, Sawyer, Finch, Treby and Holt, for their opinions.[2] Five questions were put to the counsel:

1. *Quare* whether this surrender be agreeable to the submission of the Common Council and to the regulations required by His Majesty?

2. Whether by this surrender the office of mayoralty is surrendered?

3. If so, then whether the prescriptions and customs belonging to that office are not thereby surrendered and lost?

4. Whether in case that Judgement be entered up the consequences thereof be not more fatal than this surrender?

5. How far the regrant does confirm and restore the City to the liberties etc., therein mentioned?[3]

The most interesting parts of these opinions are those dealing with the effect of allowing the judgement given to be entered, as compared with the effect of surrendering the Charter.

The nature of the judgement asked for by the Crown was extensively discussed during the arguments on the case, and, as has been shown, the two Crown Counsel, Sawyer and Finch did not seem to agree. The City's argument was that the liberty of being a corporation could not be seized into the King's hands as he was incapable of exercising it. A corporation was a mere capacity, not a franchise, and thus incapable of being transferred. Accordingly, said the City, if any judgement of seizure is given, it must amount to a judgement of ouster, and the Corporation would thus be entirely dissolved and annulled, its debts, customs,

---

[1] Maitland, *History of London*, i, 479 ff. *London Gazette* 18th June 1683 : No. 1838.

[2] Sharpe, *London and the Kingdom*, ii, 503. *Journal of the Common Council*, vol. 50.

[3] These opinions are to be found in the Guildhall Record Office, Small MS Box 20, No. 5.

privileges extinguished, its lands returning to its donors, and having no privity with any new corporation which might be set up in its place. The City, of course, denied that such a judgement of ouster could be given either. The reason for stressing that judgement for the King could only result in the complete dissolution of the Corporation was to counter the Attorney General's suggestion that, by asking for judgement of seizure, the King did not intend to extinguish the Corporation, but merely to lay his hands 'gently' on the City and appoint a *custos* to govern it. But the form of the writ of *quo warranto* forces the Crown to allege that, however gently the King may lay his hands on the corporation, it is in fact dissolved.[4] Even so, Sawyer maintained during the trial that this did not mean that a judgement of ouster must be entered, and the City need not irrevocably lose its ancient customs. Treby could only envisage two types of judgement. Either the liberties are seized, (which was the position when the *custodes* were placed over London and other cities in the reigns of Edward I, II and III, and Richard II), or the entire corporation is forfeit and finally dissolved by judgement of ouster. Sawyer contended that there is no such distinction between seizure and forfeiture. Liberties could be placed into the King's hands if the party in whom they are vested misuses them. The defendant could then appear to replevin them, but if he defaulted or lost then the judgement of seizure became a final one of forfeiture. The form of this final judgement may be either of seizure or of ouster. The only difference between them was that ouster is given where the liberties have been usurped on no title at all, and seizure is where the liberty was originally validly granted but was then misused. Where the liberties are seized the King can regrant them, but not where they have been ousted, there being no valid right which can be regranted. Thus Sawyer contended that although the Corporation is dissolved by seizure, the King could nevertheless regrant it and it would have privity with, and all the old customs of, the old Corporation.

These differences of opinion as to the effect of the judgement

4 See below, p. 67.

became more apparent in the opinions given to the City in answer to the questions on their draft surrender. Sawyer remained of the same opinion as at the trial, considering that the results of entering the judgement would be far more grave than if the City were to surrender. Finch considered that the judgement was one of ouster, which is also consistent with his argument in the case itself. Holt, a Whig sympathiser, who nevertheless always considered that it was possible for corporations to be forfeited by the King was also asked for his opinion. He considered that the effect of the judgement would be to annul the corporation completely. Nothing except an Act of Parliament or a reversal of the judgement on a writ of error could revive the franchises and estates of the City.[5] If judgement is entered, the Corporation is dissolved and the consequences would be much worse than if the Charter were to be surrendered.

On first sight it would seem as though Treby's advice to the City was rather quixotic, in view of the dire consequences that, in his argument in the case, he foretold would result from judgement for the King. He advised the City that to surrender under the King's conditions would be far more disastrous than to await the entry of judgement. He maintained that the form of the judgement *quod libertas capiatur*—that the liberty of the City be taken into the King's hands—was exactly the same as those of the old precedents cited by the Crown. Accordingly, the effect must be the same, which was merely that the King placed a *custos* over the City to govern it. This *custos* always took the same oaths as the Mayor, to preserve the liberties and customs of the City. When the *custos* was appointed there was no loss of lands, offices or liberties and the business of the Corporation went on as usual. London would not be reduced to a village by this judgement, but would revert to normal as soon as the *custos* was taken off. The surrender, on the other hand, would mean that the whole nature of the government

[5] This is consistent with his judgement in *R. v. City of London* (1692) Holt 168, where he says that the right of being a body politic is incapable of subsisting in the King for it is a liberty which can only subsist in those persons to whom it is granted. Therefore, any judgement of seizure must necessarily dissolve the corporation for ever.

of the City would be altered for ever, for if the mayoralty and commonalty are surrendered, the corporation would be dissolved. All the officers would be appointed by the King and all the power would be held by men under Royal control. The City would be a mere tenant at will of their rights and franchises. The Mayor would hold office solely by virtue of Royal appointment, and thus all his rights, now claimed by prescription, would be lost, as his title would no longer rest on prescription. The other counsel, said Treby, had used the fear of dissolution by judgement to induce surrender. But if the corporation were surrendered to the King, there would be nothing to prevent him from subsequently dissolving it. The judgement could not dissolve it, and to execute in such a fashion would found a writ of error. This is the reason why the King would be more gratified by surrender than by entering up the judgement; it would give him more power over the City.

Sawyer, Finch and Holt consider that all that is lost by the surrender is the right to choose a Mayor and other officers, and that none of the customs and prescriptions appertaining to those offices would be lost. These depend on the City's Constitution and cannot be said to be surrendered simply by the surrender of the right to choose the Mayor. By the King's regrant, the City would be in exactly the same position as now, save for the actual changes made by the King.

Despite the fact that the Common Council had accepted the King's conditions and had voted to surrender the charter on 20 June 1683, the Councillors refused to seal the draft deed of the City's surrender when it was laid before them in September, with a majority of eighteen.[6] The debate was long and acrimonious, based on the opinions of the counsel. It seems that Treby's reasons prevailed, although he was much attacked during the debate. The Duke of York reported that when the judgement was entered and the King had begun to settle the government of the City, those who had opposed the surrender were angry with

[6] Sharpe, iii, 501; the figures were 103 against, 85 for surrender. *Journal*, 50, Fol. 98.

themselves and Treby.[7] Judgement was entered against the City on 4 October 1683, and London was governed without a charter from that date until October 1688. The Court was triumphant: 'The King of England is likewise King of London' said Jeffreys.[8]

HISTORY OF LONDON 1683-8

The City was then governed by a Royal Commission, all officers being appointed by the King to act during his pleasure. Pritchard, later followed by Tulse, was immediately sworn in as Lord Mayor and Daniel and Dashwood were sworn in as Sheriffs. Treby was replaced by Jenner as Recorder and eight Whig Aldermen were dismissed and replaced. The King appointed sixteen Justices of the Peace.[9] No Common Council sat from December 1683 until the liberties were restored in 1688. The governing body of the City was the Court of Aldermen, but in fact it seems that Jeffreys had the real power, the Mayor and Aldermen having to approach him before they could get to the King.[10] Many officers were rather alarmed at the strange way in which the government of the City was being carried on.[11] North alleged, however, that the citizens would have noticed no difference in the effectiveness of the government, save for the better, after the Charter was gone.[12]

Revenues and lands previously owned by the City were leased by the King to certain Aldermen on trust, although, according to the law, the lands should have reverted to the donors if in fact the corporation was dissolved. A number of sources of income were lost as a result of the judgement. A petition was addressed to the King saying that, of the revenue leased to the Aldermen, certain fines and forfeitures arising from the Courts of Conservancy for

[7] *Cal.S.P.Dom.* 1683/4, Oct. 5, p. 13.

[8] Burnet, *History of My Own Time*, p. 397.

[9] Maitland, *History of London*, i, 483; Sharpe, op. cit., ii, 504 ff.; *Cal.S.P.Dom.* 1683/4, p. 16.

[10] Reresby, *Memoirs*, p. 308.

[11] *Cal.S.P.Dom.* 1683/4, p. 39.

[12] It is interesting to see how the trust was used to confer those advantages, such as perpetual succession, previously obtained by incorporation.

the Thames had not been expressly included and the City's officers prayed that they should be included. Some of these revenues had been granted to the Earl of Clarendon and complaints that he had encroached on the Conservancy led to the ordering of a *scire facias* against him.[13] The leases were periodically renewed. In 1685 the Mayor and Aldermen asked for a renewal and requested that certain revenues be particularly enumerated, such as tronage, package, scavage, bailliage and portage, as they had not been expressly included in the former grant.[14] One of the causes for the City's bankruptcy in 1693 was said to be this loss, but the financial state of the City had been perilous long before the case. Nevertheless, the City did lose some revenues, such as the profits of the King's Beam, Stillyard Beam, waterbailliage duties, tronage etc. Also, the costs of the case had been heavy and the City's credit diminished.[15]

It is a little difficult to fathom the exact nature of the legal position of the City during these years. If the Corporation was dissolved, as was generally thought, its lands ought to have reverted to the donors, and the administrators ought to have been legally free of all obligations contracted by the Corporation before 1683. But the land remained and the obligations were honoured. Also, if the Corporation was entirely dissolved, James could not have revived it in 1688 by Proclamation. (He could, of course, have incorporated a new corporation.) Quite apart from these points, there is no record of any execution of the judgement having been issued. Following a judgement of seizure on a *quo warranto*, a writ of seizure should be issued to the sheriff, though this writ has been omitted in other cases besides that of London.[16] Clearly times were arbitrary and no satisfactory explanation of the City's legal status can be given. It appears to be very like the situation in the days of Henry III, Edward I, and Richard II, when the City was placed under *custos*, and thus in practice, it

[13] Luttrell, *A Brief Historical Relation of State Affairs*, i, 302–3, 417.

[14] *Cal.S.P.Dom.* 1685, No. 564.

[15] Kellett, 'The Causes of the Financial Decline of the City of London', p. 156. Pamphlet, 'The Cities Case' (1693).

[16] See Kyd, *Law of Corporations*, ii, 509 on *quo warrantos*.

seems that Treby's view of the effect of the judgement was right.[17] It is not surprising, however, that the City wanted an Act of Parliament to restore their charter, rather than to rely on James's Proclamation.

At first the Mayor and Aldermen were denied their customary honours at James II's coronation because of the loss of the franchise, but eventually the King allowed them.[18] For the 1685 election, the King authorised the Court of Aldermen to grant liveries to certain Companies for the purpose of voting, but only if they were of unquestionable loyalty.[19] Accordingly twelve Companies were ordered to select a certain number of liverymen, to be approved by the Court of Aldermen. In consequence, four Tory Aldermen were returned to Parliament.[20] During 1686 there were serious anti-Catholic riots in the City, which the Mayor had difficulty in subduing. The Army established a camp at Hounslow to aid the King if necessary.[21] James turned to the dissenters for allies, including them in the Declaration of Indulgence. In many of the London Livery Companies, the Tories who had replaced the Whigs were in turn replaced by dissenters. The Court of Aldermen, half of which was already appointed by the King, refused to send an address of thanks for the Declaration of Indulgence, and therefore had to be further 'remodelled'. The King declared that in future only he should nominate Aldermen as vacancies occurred. Those who refused to serve would be fined. The City collected £8500 in fines,[22] many Aldermen resigning because they did not wish to vote an address of thanks for the Declaration. The Court was eventually sufficiently filled with dissenters to pass the address (July 1687). In October, Sir John Shorter, a well-known Anabaptist, was appointed Lord Mayor by letters patent.

On 6 October 1688, in the face of the invitation to the Prince of Orange and the disaffection of the troops at Hounslow, James restored the City Liberties as fully as before the *Quo Warranto*.[23] A

---

[17] Above, p. 53.   [18] Repertory 90, Fol. 61; Sharpe, op. cit., ii, 508

[19] *Journal*, 50, Fol. 135; Repertory 90, Fol. 80.

[20] Sharpe, op. cit., ii, 509.

[21] Luttrell, op. cit., i, 373–5, 378.   [22] Sharpe, op. cit., ii, 519.

[23] *London Gazette*, No. 2388, Oct. 1688.

Mayor and Sheriffs were appointed, and those officers who had held posts before the Case, including Treby, were re-appointed.[24] On the following day, a Sunday, a special Court of Aldermen was held to restore the Livery Companies to their pre-1683 position and re-appoint the deprived liverymen.[25] The Court also presented a guarded and cool address to the King.[26] A new Common Council was elected in November 1688 and Parliamentary Writs issued. Nevertheless the King was unable to win back the support of the City, and the House of Lords was permitted to sit in the Guildhall in order to make a declaration in favour of William. The Common Council assured him of a welcome reception, and he received every co-operation from London when he landed.

The four well-known Whigs, Ward, Clayton, Pilkington and Love, who had represented the City in Charles II's reign, were elected to the Convention Parliament. A special Committee of the House of Commons, set up to examine the City grievances, reported that the judgement on the *Quo Warranto* was illegal and that the City's rights in the election of sheriffs in 1682 had been illegally invaded. The Common Council also set up a Committee to obtain the reversal of the judgement and they produced a draft bill. Accordingly, an Act [27] was passed in 1690 restoring the City to its ancient rights, and enacting that the City might prescribe to be a corporation. The Act declared that the judgement was 'illegal and arbitrary', and provided that the Charter of the City of London should never henceforward be forfeited for any cause whatsoever. Thus the City is now safe from any further *quo warranto* or *scire facias* action against its Charter. As it probably cannot surrender itself (being a corporation by prescription),[28] the only method by which the Corporation of the City of London could be dissolved, apart from by Act of Parliament, would be by the death of, or a refusal to act by, its members.

The dispute over London's charter concluded with the case of

---

[24] Sharpe, op. cit., ii, 531; Maitland, op. cit., i, 485.
[25] Maitland, op. cit., p. 485–6.   [26] Sharpe, op. cit., ii, 530–1.
[27] 2 Will & Mar., c. 8 (1690).
[28] See pp. 104–5.

R. v. *City of London* (1692),[29] but the judges in this case neatly avoided having to decide on the legality of the *Quo Warranto* judgement. The facts were as follows. James Smith was an alderman of the City at the time of the *Quo Warranto* and after the judgement he lost his office. The Act of 1690 abrogated all charters and letters patent granted to the City after the judgement and reinstated all those who had rightfully held office before it. Smith resumed his office. However, Statute 1 William and Mary enacted that any person then holding any military or civil office must take oaths before August 1689, or vacate the office, and Smith had not taken these oaths. Was he entitled to the office of Alderman? The question depended on the effect of the *Quo Warranto* judgement. If it dissolved the corporation, then Smith was not an alderman in August 1689, there being no corporation of which to be an alderman, and, therefore, he was not liable to take the oaths required by the Statute. If the judgement did not dissolve the corporation, Smith had in effect remained an alderman throughout and therefore was liable to take the oaths as he was the holder of a civil office at the time when the 1689 Statute was passed. This case would seem to present an ideal opportunity for an authoritative judicial pronouncement on the effect of a *quo warranto* judgement. Unfortunately, the defendant's return did not recite the judgement as entered on the Court Record but used the version which was recited in the 1690 Act. This was 'that the liberty, franchise, and privilege of the City of London, being a body politic etc., should be seized'. It did not say that the liberty *of* being a body politic should be seized, which is how it appeared on the Court Record. The Court had no difficulty in deciding that the judgement as recited in the Act was a seizure of the franchises, but not a seizure of the body politic itself. Holt did not doubt that a corporation could be seized but said that a judgement of seizure could not achieve this. A corporation can only be dissolved, he considered, by a judgement of ouster.

[29] (1692) Holt 168.

CHAPTER V

The Legality of the London Decision

I. CAN A CORPORATION BE DISSOLVED?

IT IS now accepted that corporations can be forfeited, but the position in 1683 was doubtful. The case could, quite legitimately, have been decided for either party, and therefore the fact that the judgement for the Crown was obtained by manipulating the appointment of judges to the King's Bench, and by considerable Royal activity behind the scenes, does not mean that the case is devoid of points of interest and difficulty to lawyers. Despite the disfavour with which the Stuart intervention in the constitution of the boroughs has been held since 1688, the view of the law put forward by the Crown in the London Case is now considered to be correct. Unfortunately, the brevity of the actual judgement makes it useless in any discussion of the legal basis of the decision.

(a) *The Law at 1683*

The Crown could cite no considered judgement which was exactly the same as that claimed in the London Case, that is, the forfeiture of the Charter for abusing its powers by means of the *quo warranto*. A great many cases were cited which occurred in the reigns of James I and Charles I.[1] As none of these were reported, it is impossible to tell whether they were cases of forfeiture for abuser, or of ouster for usurping to be a corporation without title, the writ of *quo warranto* being the same in both cases. However, whatever they were is irrelevant in that all of them resulted either in the entry of a *nolle prosequi* (at the surrender of the town in question), or in judgement being given by default. Thus, as none of them provide a considered judgement on a contested case, they

---

[1] See footnotes 60 and 63 of Chapter 3, pp. 39 and 40.

cannot be said to be conclusive authority for the Crown, though they do indicate that charters had been forfeited before,[2] and, as Finch pointed out, it would be strange if a charter could be forfeited where a party defaulted, yet could not be forfeited where an abuse had been pleaded to and upheld by the Court.[3] Of these more recent cases, only that of *New Malton* came to judgement, and that was a case of usurping to be a corporation without good title, and not of abusing the charter. Pollexfen distinguished the case on this ground,[4] but he put this point last, as if it was not particularly important. Neither side in the case stressed the distinction between abusing a valid charter and usurping a right to be incorporated without a valid charter. The form of the Writ was more appropriate to the latter situation, as it demanded to know by what warrant the defendants claimed to be incorporated. Sawyer, however, uses cases of usurper as direct authorities in maintaining that charters of incorporation could be forfeited for abuser. He says that the cases cited by the City to show that the action should have been brought against individuals and not in the name of the corporation, show also that corporations *can* be forfeited. But in fact all the cases cited by Treby in this respect are cases of usurping, and not abusing, a charter of incorporation.[5]

Sawyer and Finch relied more heavily on the older authorities, and these cases do seem to be strongly in their favour. They all concerned towns where the liberties were seized and the government taken over by the King, because of some offence committed by them.[6] However, none of these seizures were effected by the writ of *quo warranto*. Some of them are examples of the use of a direct criminal indictment against a corporation. In the case of Winchester[7] the Mayor and Bailiffs had allowed a hostage to escape and the City was indicted before Parliament. Judgement was

---

[2] See for examples above, pp. 11–16.

[3] *S.T.*, viii, 1090; it is now considered that a corporation cannot be finally forfeited in default of appearance: *R.* v. *Amery* (1786) 2 T.R. 515.

[4] For Pollexfen's other, equally valid, objections to this case, see above, pp. 39–40.

[5] *Helmsley*, Co. Ent. 527; *Musician's Case*, T.21, Car. r. 18; *Cusak*, Palmer 1.

[6] See above, pp. 31–2.

[7] 33 E.1; *Placita Parliamenti*, 277.

that the Mayor, Bailiffs and six other citizens should be imprisoned for the community default, and that the liberties of the City should be seized into the King's hands. Later, on payment of a fine, the liberties were restored. The City of Norwich[8] was indicted for riot, treason and a host of other trespasses, and their liberties were seized. The cases of London, Sandwich, Cambridge and Oxford were similarly direct proceedings for crimes. In his book on the *quo warrantos* of Edward I Mr Sutherland gives examples of only three occasions in which a town's liberties were seized for usurping or abusing franchises.[9] These were not cited by the Crown. There are many cases where the liberties of a corporation were seized for non-payment of taxes, which the Crown does not cite, for some unknown reason. Madox[10] gives a multitude of authorities showing this up to the time of Henry VII, but again these were not examples of *quo warrantos*, and cannot be said to be direct authority for the Crown, though they are very persuasive.

The City's objections to these cases carry considerable weight. The cases are old and of a political nature occurring in very unsettled times. More important is the fact that the corporations were not regarded as dissolved as a result of the judgements. The business of the corporations continued, and many of them, after they had been restored to their status by the King, still claimed to be corporations by prescription.[11] Had they been entirely dissolved, they would have had to be reincorporated by charter and therefore their title would no longer rest upon prescription, which presumes that a Royal grant of incorporation had been lost before the time of living memory.[12]

An important objection to these cases, for which the above points of the City is evidence, is that, at the time at which most of them were decided, the law of corporate personality had not been

[8] M. Communa 23 Hen. 6, r. 35.

[9] *Wigan, Plac. Q.W.* 371–3; *Lancaster, Plac.Q.W.* 384; *Preston, Plac. Q.W.* 385; Sutherland, *Quo Warranto Proceedings in the Reign of Edward I* (1964), p. 160.

[10] *Firma Burgi*, pp. 161–4.

[11] See above, p. 36.

[12] A corporation can only be created by the King, either expressly, or, in the case of ancient corporations, by the fiction that the Royal grant had been lost.

worked out and any cases from this period should be treated circumspectly.[13] The City says that the most recent of the Crown's cases is that of London in 1393 (16 R.2). This is not accurate, as the seizure of Norwich's liberties for treason took place in Henry VI's reign in 1445. Also, these cases cited by Madox (but not used by the Crown in the case) of the seizure of liberties for non-payment of taxes continued up to the reign of Henry VII. But it is true that most of the authorities belong to the era before Richard II, and that there are few examples of corporations being indicted for crimes after that time. Can any of these boroughs be regarded as incorporated at the time when the cases were decided? The question of when the boroughs were incorporated has been disputed. Merewether and Stephens declare that not until the reign of Henry VI did the charters conferred on the boroughs incorporate them, as only then was a certain form of words used which could confer true incorporation. Their conclusion from this is, of course, that there can be no corporation by prescription as there was in fact no charter of incorporation granted before the time of living memory. This view has been attacked as paying excessive attention to form and documentary evidence.[14] Gross [15] suggests that in essence some municipal corporations existed as early as the reign of Edward I, but the word incorporation was not used until the reign of Edward III. The earliest charter conferring incorporation, as compared to those merely conferring certain privileges on a collection of individuals, had been said to be that conferred on Wells in 1343.[16]

In any case, whenever it happened, formal incorporation seemed to make little difference to those boroughs that had it. Non-incorporated bodies enjoyed privileges and also perpetual succession.[17] Wang quotes many examples of unincorporated bodies being treated as a single unit. For example, the unincorporated town of Baston in 9 R.2 was sued in that name and judgement

---

[13] The City itself did not make this point.

[14] Carr, C. T., *Law of Corporations* (Cambridge, 1905), p. 129.

[15] *Guild Merchant*, i, p. 93.

[16] Wang, 'The Incorporate Person' (Ph.D. Thesis, London, 1942).

[17] Madox, *Firma Burgi*, p. 49.

given 'quod villata de Baston exoneretur'. He concludes that up to the beginning of the fifteenth century the significance of incorporation was not clear. 'It appears to be no more than machinery to obtain favours from the King. . . . Groups of men continue to act as a unit whether incorporated or not.' Certainly the personality of the borough was not regarded as separated from the personality of individual burgesses. In 1345 a bond was given by the Mayor and Commonalty of Newcastle to its Mayor. It was held that it was void as a man could not give a bond to himself.[18] In 1424, it was held that a member of a corporation could not appear as its attorney as it would be the equivalent of appearing for himself.[19] It is true that a separate corporate personality was emerging at this time for other purposes. During the reign of Henry IV it was held that a fee simple could be validly conveyed to a corporation without the addition of the words 'and his heirs'. One of the most important discussions in the Year Books on the nature of the corporate borough appears in 1482, the *Abbot of Hulme's Case*, which has been carefully examined by Mr Lubasz.[20] He points out that the borough changed from being a vague *communitas* by the end of the thirteenth century, to become a corporation with clearly defined characteristics by the end of the fifteenth century. The decision is not reported in the *Abbot of Hulme's Case*, but the arguments show the kind of problem that was beginning to be recognised. How far were the powers of a corporation separate from the powers of the individuals comprising it? Did the imprisonment of the Mayor mean that a bond executed by the Corporation of Norwich (which of course included the Mayor) was void for duress? The law on corporate personality was in a state of flux at the time when these seizures occurred, and the question of whether a corporation was entirely dissolved by the deprivation of its franchises was not a question that was considered. It would be inappropriate to try to

---

[18] YB. 17 & 18 Ed. 3 (RS) 70; Holdsworth, *History of English Law*, i, 482.

[19] YB. 3 Hen. 6, pl. 16; Holdsworth, op. cit., i, 482. See Pollock and Maitland, *History of the Common Law*, i, 493.

[20] 80 L.Q.R. 228 (1964).

fit these cases into the more sophisticated notions of corporate personality which developed later. Many of Sawyer's authorities, such as those of Winchester and Cambridge, were decided before the borough could be said to be incorporated.

Textbook and statutory authority for forfeiture was as inconclusive as the case law on the subject in 1683. The City is correct in alleging that in no textbook or case is it suggested that the *Statute de Quo Warranto* and its amending measures could be used for dissolving corporations for abusing their franchises. For instance, in the *Natura Brevium*,[21] the *quo warranto* is said to lie where a person usurps certain franchises, such as waifs, felon's goods or markets, without title. Coke[22] uses the same examples. Under the Statute of Gloucester,[23] whereby Sheriffs were to summons all who claimed franchises to show good title, there is no record that a corporation had to show good title to be a body corporate, or that such a charter was seized for abuse. It is also significant that Henry VIII did not use these statutes to dissolve the ecclesiastical corporations. But Brook,[24] under the heading 'Corporations and Franchises', says that a patent from the King can be declared void by a *scire facias* if it is abused, and a charter of incorporation is a patent from the King. As has already been noted, the use of the *quo warranto* to deprive a corporation of its charter had occurred to James I in 1628–9.[25] Cromwell had also desired to regulate corporations but did not use this method. A member of his Committee on Corporations, William Sheppard, wrote the first treatise dealing exclusively with corporation law.[26] On the dissolution of corporations he merely says, 'a corporation may be dissolved by Parliament. And it seems it may not be dissolved otherwise.' Elsewhere, dealing with abuses of corporate power, he writes:

If any corporation shall oppress any of the people under their power, by imposition of unjust rates, the making and execution of unreasonable

---

[21] Fol. LXXVIII.   [22] 2 Inst. 278.   [23] (1278) 6 Ed. 1.
[24] Brooke, Sir R., *Abridgement* (London, 1586), Part II, f. 125.
[25] See above, p. 12.
[26] Sheppard, W., *Of Corporations* (1659).

ordinances . . . the party grieved hereby may have his relief by complaint to the Upper Bench.

This does not suggest that the corporation would be thereby dissolved and it would thus seem that any such power was unrecognised, and even unconsidered, at that time. The City cites a number of statutes[27] which impose fines on corporations for abusing their right to make by-laws, and asks why these should be necessary if the corporations could be forfeited by a *quo warranto* for the same offence? The Crown replied that those statutes applied only to guilds, and not to borough corporations. 15 Henry 6, chapter 6 recites that, 'the masters, wardens, and people of the guilds, fraternities and other companies incorporated' must register their by-laws before a Justice of the Peace or the governors of the cities or boroughs in which the guilds etc., are situated or pay a fine. This certainly indicates that the boroughs were not to be regarded as 'other companies incorporate', and in any case it could be argued that the provision of lesser penalties for the abuse of a charter does not necessarily infer the non-existence of the ultimate penalty, forfeiture.

The Crown produced two statutes[28] which show that corporations can be forfeited, and they seem to be very strong authorities. The liberties of the City of London were seized under the statute 28 Edward 3 chapter 10 in the time of Richard II.[29] However, though this shows that the liberties might be seized, the fact remains that the crown was suing in 1683 by means of the writ of *quo warranto* in the King's Bench, and not by virtue of that statute[30] (which provides for a special commission to hear the case). In any case the City denied, on the grounds mentioned before, that such a seizure dissolved the corporation.

It might be wondered why the Crown did not sue the

---

[27] 15 Hen. 6, c. 6; 12 Hen. 7, c. 7; 19 Hen. 7, c. 7; 22 Hen. 8, c. 4; 28 Hen. 8, c. 5.

[28] 28 Ed. 3, c. 10; 1 Hen. 4, c. 15. See above, pp. 43–4.

[29] L6 R.2, Lib.H, fol. 269b, City Register.

[30] Although amended by 1 Hen. 4, c. 15, neither seems to have been repealed in 1683.

corporation in the same way as in the old cases it cited, and thus avoid all the dispute as to whether a corporation could be dissolved and, if so, whether it could be done by a writ of *quo warranto*. The probable reason is the rather arbitrary nature of those precedents, which were really political decisions in times of great upheaval. No single procedure was adopted. Sometimes judgement was given by the King in Parliament, acting in a judicial capacity no longer possible. Other seizures were ordered by the Justices in Eyre or by special commissions. Others were effected by direct criminal indictments, and by 1683 the case of *Suttons Hospital* was very strong authority for the proposition that a corporation could not be indicted for a crime. The use of the *quo warranto* against corporations had long been the normal and satisfactory method of proceeding against them for their individual franchises, and where persons claimed without any good title to be incorporated. The threat of a *quo warranto* had been sufficient to induce surrender from those who had abused their charters, at least from the time of James I.[31] Until 1683, when all the resources of the City were used, for the first time, to examine the legal nature of *quo warrantos* and the dissolution of corporations there had been no reason to doubt the legality of questioning a charter by *quo warranto*. Thus it was to be expected that the Crown would use it against the City, especially as it was always hoped that the City would surrender. It was the very nature of the writ which forced the Crown into the position of maintaining that corporations could be dissolved completely. As James's activities showed he was not particularly interested in whether the City could be said to be completely dissolved; all he desired was to control its personnel, just as Edward III and Richard II had done, by appointing a *custos* over the City. But the writ demanded that the City should show by what warrant they acted as a body politic, and thus the Crown was required to show that, because of the offences committed, the City had no right to be a body politic.

[31] See above, pp. 11 ff.

(b) *The law after 1683*

The law on the forfeiture of corporations was thus unclear in 1683, though the Crown had the stronger case. It was still disputed immediately after the Revolution. In 1690, of the judges asked by Parliament if a corporation by prescription could forfeit its being, three said no and two (including Holt) said yes.[32] Once the heat of political controversy had died down, it was generally accepted that corporations could be dissolved.[33] As late as 1786, in *R. v. Amery*,[34] it was argued by the Crown that corporations could not be forfeited, and their reasons were the same as those of the City in 1683. It was considered that the examination of the precedents in the London Case was exhaustive, and nothing new was added. This case, however, concerned the effect of a judgement of seizure *quosque* against the Charter of Chester, and it was held by the Lords that such a judgement does not finally dissolve the Corporation. Therefore, the effect of a final judgement of seizure was not in issue. Discussing the forfeitures of charters over a century later, Kyd[35] could shed no new light on the question, and, though he considered that corporations could be dissolved, he was critical of parts of Sawyer's argument, and he approved of Pollexfen's objections to the Crown's old precedents. Only Norton and Pulling, writing on the History and customs of London in 1869 and 1842 respectively, deny the possibility of forfeiture. This opinion can probably be explained by their enthusiasm for the heritage of the City and is not supported by any examination of the Common Law.

I can only find one reported example after 1688 of the Courts forfeiting a charter of incorporation for abuse of its powers. In *Eastern Archipelago Company v. R.* (1853),[36] a *scire facias* was brought against the Company for the abuse of their charter, which was repealed. Martin B. said, 'I find it laid down that a

---

[32] *H.M.C. Rep.* 13 Pt. v, p. 70.

[33] See *R. v. City of London* (1692) Holt, 168; *City of London v. Vanacre* (1699) 12 Mod. 271; *Colchester v. Seaber* (1766) 3 Burr. 1866.

[34] (1786) 2 T.R. 515.

[35] Kyd, *Law of Corporations*, ii, 474 ff.

[36] (1853) 2 E. & B. 856 at p. 869.

corporation may be dissolved for either of these two causes, misuser or abuse, and that there is a tacit or implied condition annexed to all such grants as the present, that they shall not be abused or misused, and that, if they be, the charter or franchise is forfeited.' His authorities were *R.* v. *City of London*,[37] *City of London* v. *Vanacre*,[38] and Blackstone.

Holdsworth writes that it is now considered that a *scire facias* is more appropriate where a charter has been abused and a *quo warranto* (or information in the nature of a *quo warranto*) for usurping a corporation without title.[39] A judgement on a *quo warranto* does not necessarily dissolve the corporation for it can be regranted by the King in the same manner as he can regrant a corporation that has surrendered. A judgement on a *scire facias* finally repeals the charter. This distinction was not recognised before 1683, when the two writs were used in both situations.[40] Holdsworth considers that Treby's objection, that it is illogical to sue the Corporation on a *quo warranto* when the writ denies that the corporation has a right to exist, has helped to fix this distinction.[41] However, Grant,[42] in a very confusing chapter on the subject, concludes that the position is as follows. Where a *quo warranto* is brought against individuals for usurping the right to incorporation, a judgement of ouster is given and this does not dissolve the corporation.[43] A judgement on a *scire facias* for abuse finally dissolves the corporation. But, where it is not desired to repeal the charter, a *quo warranto* can be brought for either usurper or abuser, and a judgement of seizure, suspending the corporation, is given.[44] The corporation can then be regranted. This conclusion

[37] (1692) Holt, 168.

[38] (1699) 12 Mod. 271.

[39] *R.* v. *Passmore* (1789) 3 T.R. 241; *City of London* v. *Vanacre* (1699) 12 Mod. 271; *R.* v. *Bewdley* (1712) 1 P. Wms. 207.

[40] For instance, a *quo warranto* was issued against London, but a *scire facias* was issued against Massachusetts and an entry in *Cal. S.P.Dom.* 1681, p. 682 shows that a *scire facias* was being thought of against London.

[41] Holdsworth, op. cit., iv, 67. See above, pp. 38–40.

[42] Grant, *Law of Corporations*, p. 295.

[43] *Colchester* v. *Seaber* (1766) 3 Burr. 1866.

[44] *Peter* v. *Kendal* (1827) 6 B. & C. 703.

therefore *does* contemplate a *quo warranto* being brought against a corporation for abuser and Treby's objections presumably would not be upheld. Grant's conclusion seems correct on the basis of *Peter* v. *Kendal* where it was said: 'Proceeding by *quo warranto* supposes the party in actual, though not in legal possession, and therefore judgement of ouster is necessary to dispossess him. In the case of an abuse of a franchise by negligence, the Crown may repeal the grant by *scire facias* or *quo warranto*, and may vest it in some other person.' It was not suggested in *Eastern Archipelago Company* v. *R.* that a *quo warranto* was an alternative to the *scire facias*, however. Lack of satisfactory authority makes the position rather obscure. Though it would be logically more appropriate to use the *scire facias* only in cases of abuser, there would be practical disadvantages. Where a corporation abuses its powers, the only remedy (apart from the possibility of suing individual officers) would be to repeal the charter, involving the many inconveniences that led the judges in *Colchester* v. *Seaber*,[45] and *R.* v. *Passmore*[46] to hold that where a corporation surrenders or where all its members die, the corporation is not irrevocably dissolved but merely suspended, and capable of being regranted by the King.[47] Where a corporation is dissolved, its lands revert to the donors, its chattels to the King, and its rights and liabilities are extinguished. This disadvantage is rendered more serious because it would appear that the slightest breach of a charter is a ground for forfeiture.[48]

The *scire facias* is still the appropriate method by which charters or letters patent are annulled. In *Att-Gen.* v. *Colchester Corporation* (1955),[49] one of the grounds for not granting an injunction to enforce the Corporation to operate a ferry was that their refusal could be grounds for a *scire facias* by the Crown to repeal the charter granting the ferry. The Crown could then, if it wished, grant the ferry to some other person. However, if a charter of incorporation were repealed by *scire facias*, the old corporation

---

[45] (1766) 3 Burr. 1866.   [46] (1789) 3 T.R. 241.   [47] See below, p. 106.
[48] Blackstone, *Commentaries*, i, 484. See below, p. 71.
[49] 2 Q.B. 207.

could not be given to others, as a corporation is a right that cannot subsist in the Crown to be regranted.[50]

2. OTHER LEGAL POINTS ARISING FROM THE CASE

The question of whether or not the action should have been brought against the individual members of the corporation and not in the name of the corporation itself has already been considered. It would seem that either form was possible however illogical this would appear to be.

The City's argument, that the acts of the Common Council did not bind the Corporation, is effectively demolished by Sawyer.[51] The City was prepared to put forward every objection they could think of, even if it meant alleging that the acts of the governing body of the Corporation were not binding. Pollexfen also argues that the Common Council's act is not binding because it was not done under the Common Seal. To this Sawyer merely replies that if that were the case, then the Mayor and Sheriffs had no legal authority to act, for they were not appointed under the Common Seal—which is not really an answer to Pollexfen's point. Not until 1702[52] was it laid down that the seal was not needed for acts which were matters of record, the corporation being estopped from denying them. Sawyer did not mention estoppel, so it would seem that this point was uncertain in 1683.

The Causes of Forfeiture

What type of abuses merit the repeal of the charter by *scire facias* or seizure by *quo warranto*? In so far as the main issues raised by the London Case have been discussed at all, most authorities have restricted themselves to the question of whether it is ever possible to forfeit a charter of incorporation, and have not considered the nature of the abuses which will have this effect. In the period before the charter of 1 E.3, it appears that the City's liberties

---

[50] *R. v. City of London* (1692) Holt, 168.
[51] Above, p. 42.
[52] *Mayor of Thetford's Case.* Holdsworth, op. cit., ix, 53.

were lost on account of the personal transgressions of officers, this position being alleviated by that charter. Statute 28 E.3, c.10 as amended by 1 H.4, c.15, leaves the question of what defaults of the Mayor, Sheriffs or Aldermen should incur forfeiture of the liberties to the discretion of the judges. In 1683, the City quotes the case where the taking of a toll was declared illegal, but this did not incur the forfeiture of the market, for the market was not incident to the toll. Can the City be described as incident to its markets, that the taking of an illegal toll in them should forfeit the entire Charter? The Crown's answer to this is that the passing of the by-law to collect the tolls was an abuse of the City's lawmaking powers, and that this power is incident to its very existence as a corporation.[53] The Crown's view of the law has been accepted ever since, despite the fact that it makes the existence of corporations very precarious. In the London case the Crown clearly thought that the slightest infringement of the charter merited its forfeiture and this is considered to be the law by Blackstone.[54] There are virtually no cases on this, neither have legal writers discussed the point. In the *City of London* v. *Vanacre*[55] Holt declares that neglect to comply with the terms of a franchise would result in its repeal by a *scire facias* and that the facts in this particular case, a neglect to make an election as letters patent had appointed, had this effect. He appears to assume that any neglect at all would have forfeited the franchise. In *Eastern Archipelago Company* v. *R.*,[56] Martin B. said,

Slight deviations from the provisions of a charter would not necessarily be either an abuse or misuser of it, and would therefore be no grounds for its annulment.

He offers no guidance as to what deviations would be regarded as slight. In America the *quo warranto* can still be used to dissolve joint stock companies. In *People* v. *North River Sugar Refining Company*,[57] it was held that the action will lie only if there is grave

[53] Above, p. 47.   [54] i, 484; ii, 262–3.   [55] 12 Mod. 271; Carth. 483.
[56] (1853) 2 E. & B. 856, at p. 87.
[57] J. Smith, *Cases in the Law of Corporations* (Cambridge (Mass.), 1897), ii, 943; G. D. Hornstein, *Corporation Law and Practice* (West Pub. Co., 1959), para. 813.

misconduct which threatens the public interest. In this case an arrangement to create a monopoly by means of the trust was held sufficiently grave to dissolve the corporation for misuse of its charter. Thus the need to prove that the abuse is contrary to public policy, allied to the fact that only the Attorney General can bring such actions, prevents the dissolution of companies for trivial reasons. But the Court has a large discretion once the action has been brought.[58]

Can a Corporation commit a crime?

This aspect of corporate law has long been the subject of dispute. The City declared that a corporation could not be held responsible for the commission of a crime, firstly because it was incapable of acting maliciously, being a mere *ens rationis*, and having no mind or soul of its own; secondly, because, as it can only validly perform those acts which are within the powers given to it by its charter, it cannot be responsible for any unauthorised act.

The Corporation and Mens Rea. The Crown accused the Corporation of malice in publishing its petition, and put forward many old cases showing that corporations have been held responsible for crimes, and thus had the necessary *mens rea*.[59] Pollock and Maitland consider these cases and conclude that it was the realisation by the Courts that a borough could be punished as a unit which helped to create the distinction in the time of Edward I, between the borough and the village.[60] A borough could lose its liberties and be fined as a community, rather than as separate individuals. At that time theories of the nature of corporate personality were not applied to the boroughs. Even so, the Romanist fiction theory was known in ecclesiastical circles, but it was not considered then that the fictional personality of a corporation prevented it from being responsible for a crime. Such

---

[58] Only the Attorney-General can bring a *quo warranto* in England—*R.* v. *Ogden* (1829) 10 B. & C., 230. Such an action cannot be filed at all against persons usurping a franchise of a private nature, not connected with government.

[59] *Derby, Plac. Q.W.* 160; *York, Placit. Abbrev.* 199; *Sandwich, Placit. Abbrev.* 273.

[60] i, 679.

a conclusion was reached later by common lawyers. Finch quotes a passage from Oldratus de Ponte[61] where he writes that a corporation has a fictitious mind, and can do wrong and be punished just as a real person can. Just as a real person can die, so a fictitious person can suffer civil death.

Later, the idea that the personality of a corporation was separate from the personality of the corporators gave rise to the conclusion that the corporation had no mind of its own, and therefore could have no evil mental state. It did not have a body of its own either, and so could not be punished. This was put forward by Pigot[62] in 1482 when he said that a corporation had no substance, was invisible, and yet was a person. This is echoed by Coke in the case of *Sutton's Hospital*,[63] 'a corporation aggregate of many is invisible, immortal, and rests only in intendment and consideration of the law . . . they cannot commit treason, nor be outlawed, nor excommunicate, for they have no souls, neither can they appear in person. . . .' It is ironical that the realisation that the borough could be punished as a group was one of the factors which marked the beginning of the distinction between the corporate and the non-incorporate body, but that the denial of the criminal responsibility of corporations should mark the beginning of the more sophisticated concept of corporate law— that the personality of the corporation is distinct from that of the corporators. The position in 1683 seems uncertain. Both sides in the case could quote authorities in their favour. Subsequently the view of the City, being also the view of Coke, prevailed, and a corporation was considered to be outside the criminal law.[64] However, this led to an illogical situation. On the one hand, a corporation could not be directly indicted for a crime, but on the other, the corporation was held responsible for crimes when they formed the basis of a *quo warranto* or *scire facias*. Thus the fictional nature of a corporation appeared to prevent it from being fined,

[61] *Consilia Sive Responsa & Aureae Questiones*, f. 29.

[62] YB. 21 ED. iv f. 13.

[63] (1612) 10 Rep. 23a.

[64] Blackstone, i, approving Coke, op. cit., p. 476. Kenny, C. S., *Outline of Criminal Law*, 17th ed. (Cambridge, 1958), p. 70.

but allowed it to be dissolved, whether its offence was trivial or grave. The situation caused difficulty because as the only method of punishing corporations was to dissolve them, it was never used, the remedy being politically suspect and rather drastic. In the nineteenth century corporations were once again held to be directly indictable for their crimes, and the inconvenient logical consequences of the fiction theory were abandoned. In one case, *Edwards* v. *Midland Railway*[65] the London Case was noted. It was noted that Saunders (who drew up the pleadings in the London Case before becoming Lord Chief Justice), was:

contemplating the proposition that a corporation aggregate could be charged with maliciously publishing a libel. No doubt it may be said that the decision is, on some grounds not of the greatest weight . . .

because it was affected by political considerations as well as legal: but the Judge considered that Saunders was a great judge, and, on this point, correct.

Ultra Vires Acts. The City alleges that it could not be guilty of criminal libel, and that the illegal by-law was not a valid act, because these acts were not within the scope of their powers as set down by the charter.[66] Although the words *ultra vires* are not used, the City's contention amounts to a clear exposition of that doctrine, which only began to be worked out in the nineteenth century. It has been thought that the *ultra vires* doctrine did not apply to chartered companies.[67] Once they were created it was supposed that they had all the powers inseparably incident to a corporation, and that even if the King's charter did restrict their activities in any way, this was not binding on the corporation. This view has been convincingly attacked as being inaccurate.[68] As English Law insists that only the Sovereign has the power to create corporations, it would be surprising if it denied the

[65] (1880) 50 L.J. (Q.B.) 281.

[66] Above, p. 45.

[67] Palmer, F. B., *Company Law*, 20th ed. (London, 1959), p. 779; Carr, *Law of Corporations*, p. 124; *Ashbury Carriage Co.* v. *Riche* (1875) L.R. 9 Ex. at p. 263.

[68] 26 L.Q.R. 320, Carden, 'Limitations on the Powers of Common Law Corporations'; Grant, *Law of Corporations*, p. 13.

Sovereign the power to restrict their activities. The London Case provides more evidence, which was not noted by Carden and his supporters, that the *ultra vires* acts of chartered corporations are invalid. The City's argument amounts to the contention that the grounds for the forfeiture are *ultra vires* and therefore void, and as such cannot affect the corporation. The Crown's reply to this gives no support to any idea that chartered corporations have unlimited powers. It is difficult to imagine Sawyer, with his horror of the all-powerful corporations forming independent groups within the Kingdom, ever proposing such an idea. He does not allege that the by-law is valid because all corporations have the power to make by-laws, but that, being unauthorised, it is a ground for forfeiture. He consistently maintains that it is illegal, being outside the terms of the charter. Thus both sides in the case appear to assume that a corporation's powers can be effectively restricted by the Crown when granting incorporation, and that they cannot validly act outside those powers.

3. THEORIES OF CORPORATE PERSONALITY

In the absence of any incontrovertible authorities on the forfeiture of corporations, the London Case provided a battle-ground for such theories of corporate personality as existed at the time, which were the fiction theory and the concession theory.

English Law is said not to follow dogmatically any theory of corporate personality, but in general to incline towards the fiction theory.[69] The basis of the fiction theory is that 'real personality' can only belong to a human being, and that when the power to act as one being is given by the law to a collection of human beings, this personality is essentially fictitious. Thus a corporation is not a real organism, but merely a legal formula. This theory has important practical implications. The personality of the corporation is entirely separated from that of the individual members.

[69] Maitland, *Introduction to Gierke: Genossenschaftsrecht*, p. xiv.

The subject of the right does not exist in the individual members thereof (nor even in all the members taken collectively) but in the ideal whole.[70]

The corporation has no mind or will of its own, and can only do those things authorised by its charter. It rests entirely upon the law. Thus it has been said,

The backbone of the fiction theory, which defines the juristic person as a *persona ficta*, is really the famous concession theory, according to which the juristic person is a concession or creation of the State.[71]

The basis of the concession theory is that all privileges and property primarily belong to the King, and that only he can concede the right to them. Accordingly, only he can grant the right to be a body politic. This theory arose from the deep suspicion with which all corporations were held in England.[72] Many of the old guilds and trading companies were disliked because of their exclusiveness and their commercial monopoly. Corporations, with their right to make laws and regulate the activities of their members, were seen as constituting a threat to the sovereignty of the state, tending to undermine the loyalty of the subjects to the King. Henry VIII fully realised the danger of ecclesiastical corporations. It is significant that the greater part of the opposition to the Monarchy during the Civil War came from the borough corporations. Far from being seen as the repositories of democracy and the bulwarks of the Constitution, as the apologists of the City in 1683 saw them,[73] the borough corporations were seen as little independent 'commonwealths' within the State, threatening its stability. Hobbes wrote,

Another infirmity of a Commonwealth . . . is the great number of corporations: which are as it were many lesser commonwealths in the bowels of a greater, like worms in the entrails of a natural man.[74]

[70] Savigny, quoted in Hallis, *Corporate Personality*, p. 9.
[71] ibid., p. 11.
[72] Carr, op. cit., pp. 164 ff.
[73] Hunt, 'A Defence of the Charter of London' (1682); 'A Modest Inquiry into the Election of Sheriffs' (1682).
[74] Hobbes, T., *Leviathan* (Collier Edn., New York, 1962), p. 245.

There is justification for this attitude in the case of the City. It had, by hard bargaining with successive monarchs, become a corporation with its own governing body, a power to make laws, hold Courts, take tolls, and enjoy a multitude of customs which in many cases were contrary to the Common Law. Other corporations had similar, if less extensive, privileges. To deny the King the right to control these bodies would considerably derogate from his sovereignty.

In the controversy as to whether or not English Law has received the fiction theory, the concession theory has always been treated as an integral part of that theory. In the London Case, the theory forcibly advocated by the City was the fiction theory, and the theory used by the Crown was the concession theory. Far from being different aspects of the same theory, the case showed that the logical consequences of the two theories conflict. The City, following Coke in the case of *Suttons Hospital*, maintains that the corporation is immortal, invisible, and rests only on intendment of law. It is a mere *ens rationis* and cannot commit a crime, for it has no mind. It can only do those acts which are authorised by its charter, and therefore cannot be responsible for an illegal act. The Crown emphatically rejects the fiction theory. Says Sawyer,

If any learned men have used such hyperbolical expressions (such as '*ens rationis*') most certainly they never intended the Citizens of London, or other populous Town or City within England, of whom the question is, but of some Corporation in Utopia, where the Citizens neither eat, drink, nor die, or at least of some Corporation that never had other existence but in the Brain.[75]

A corporation is composed of human beings who have been given the right to act as a corporation. It can only act through its human members. The privileges of acting as a body politic is a right held by each member, says Sawyer, the corporation being the sum total of those rights. That this is his view is made evident by the use he makes of *James Bagg's Case*.[76] This is directly opposed to the fiction theory, but the rejection of the fiction theory does not

[75] S.T., viii, 1161.   [76] (1616) 11 Co. 98; above, p. 33.

mean that Sawyer rejects the concession theory. Sawyer's whole argument is based on the concession theory. A corporation is created by the Crown for certain purposes and with certain powers, such as good government, and if the members in whom this right is vested abuse it, the King can take it away. Sawyer and Finch express all the fear of corporations that gave rise to the concession theory. If they could not be forfeited, they would be outside the control of the Common Law, and life in such corporations would be unsafe.

The logical application of the fiction theory would leave corporations in the powerful position that was so feared. The corporations would be immune from criminal or tortious proceedings, and would not be liable if their officers acted outside their powers. Treby shows this very clearly. His argument amounts to saying that a corporation can do no wrong because it is inconceivable that its charter would give it the power to do wrong. The concession theory necessarily demands that a corporation can do wrong. It is a part of the theory that what the King grants, he can, by due process of law, take away.[77]

The result of the case was a win for the concession theory over the fiction theory. The surrender of charters which followed the case marks the absolute triumph of the theory. Even though, in his judgement, Jones gave no appraisal of the merits of the arguments, he did feel constrained to point out the dangers of 'little republics' springing up over the Kingdom if corporations could not be forfeited. This is the view which has been subsequently followed. In 1690 Brady pours ridicule on those to whom the boroughs 'seem to have been Aeternal, or at least Coeval with the Creation'.[78] Blackstone and Kyd agree. Holdsworth also quotes Sawyer's opinion with approval, and in it he finds a moral for the twentieth century:

The failure to recognise this principal in the case of Trade Unions of workmen or masters, and the abandonment by the State of any control

[77] The King cannot deprive persons of rights by charter alone. *Hayward* v. *Fulcher* (1628), Palmer, 491.

[78] Brady, *Historical Treatise on Cities and Boroughs*, preface.

over their activities, have shown that Sir Robert Sawyer was a true prophet; for the abandonment by the State of its sovereignty has in effect set up a new feudalism, which is every whit as retrogressive as the feudalism of the Middle Ages.[79]

The fiction theory received a blow from the result of the London Case, and, in view of the fact that all the important points put forward by the Crown in the Case have subsequently been accepted by lawyers, this is cogent evidence that the theory was never really received into English Law.[80]

CONCLUSIONS

The London Case has largely been ignored by writers on the law of corporations and their history, on the grounds that the decision is of political rather than legal interest. Although Merewether and Stephens call it the 'most important case in English History', its legal implications have not been studied by lawyers.[81] Pollock,[82] writing on the history of the fiction theory of corporate personality in English Law, proposed to 'skip the great controversy in the case of the liberties of the City of London, in which there was more of politics than of law'. Kyd, in 1793, gave considerable attention to the case, but, apart from a small piece in Holdsworth, the case has not been studied subsequently. Obviously the Case was of immense political importance for it, and the surrenders of the boroughs which it precipitated, were one of the major causes of the 1688 Revolution. Nevertheless the legal issues raised in the Case are of genuine interest and difficulty. There is only one other seventeenth-century case which gives such an insight into the law of corporations at that time—the case of *Sutton's Hospital*— which is much more well known. In the London *quo warranto*

[79] Holdsworth, op. cit., ix, 46–8.

[80] Pollock, 27 *L.Q.R.* 223; he maintains that the fiction theory was never received by English Law, but he largely ignores the London Case, going straight from an examination of *Sutton's Hospital* (1612) to Blackstone's *Commentaries* for his evidence.

[81] It is scarcely mentioned in Carr, *Law of Corporations*, or H. A. Smith, *Law of Associations*.

[82] 27 *L.Q.R.* 223.

such issues as the liability of corporations for crimes and other wrongs, their responsibility for the acts of their officers, their creation and dissolution were all comprehensively argued, at a time when the law of corporations was just emerging from its medieval origins to its modern form.

The two main reasons for the Case's legal obscurity are, first, the lack of reasoned judgement which could be considered or followed in later cases. Secondly, the political events which surrounded the Case made any subsequent attempts to dissolve a corporation by means of the *quo warranto* politically suspect and therefore it was never done. Now that the most important companies are registered, and not incorporated by charter, their dissolution is regulated by Statute, and the *quo warranto* or *scire facias* has been in practice superseded.

CHAPTER VI

The Surrenders in the Country after 1683

EVEN before the judgement was given in London, provincial corporations began to surrender their charters. Thetford was the first to surrender, in December 1681. This surrender was opposed by the majority of the corporation but the pro-Court Mayor managed to get it agreed to by packing the Common Council (including his son, aged 16, in the vote) and excluding those burgesses who were against it. The new charter excluded the burgesses from the Parliamentary franchise.[1] Evidently it was generally expected that the King would win the London Case. As can be seen from the Appendix many of the new charters were granted in 1684/5 and 1685/6, but surrender and renewals continued until October 1688 when, at the very last moment, James tried to regain popular favour by restoring to the boroughs their ancient charters. The method by which the surrenders were obtained caused much offence. The King's favourites, or those who desired to become Royal favourites, would travel around the Country 'inducing' the towns to surrender, in order to advance themselves at court. The Earl of Bath had great success in Devon and Cornwall, returning from his expedition empowered to surrender fifteen charters.[2] Sunderland obtained the surrenders of the Warwickshire charters and the Earl of Yarmouth induced surrenders in Norfolk. Jeffreys obtained the surrender of many northern corporations. Even the Royalist North was shocked at the methods used. The aim was, he wrote,

either to court or frighten harmless or orderly corporations to surrender —or upon refusal, to plunge them in the chargeable and defenceless

---

[1] See Appendix A; Merewether and Stephens, *History of the Boroughs and Municipal Corporations*, iii, 1835; 10 *H. of C. Journals*, 139; *Cal.S.P. Dom.* 1680–1, p. 612.

[2] Merewether and Stephens, op. cit., p. 1794.

condition of going to law against the Crown—whereby that which could not come by fair means, was extorted by violence.[3]

By the time of James II, North considered that 'the trade of charters ran to excess and turned to an avowed practice of garbling the corporations for the purpose of carrying elections to Parliament'.[4]

It would appear that the Court followed no coherent plan of campaign in obtaining the surrenders of the borough charters. The Crown's main aim was to insure the return of loyal and reliable M.P.s and it might, therefore, be supposed that those boroughs with the strongest Whig sympathies would be first attacked. It would require a detailed analysis of the political sympathies of all the boroughs to draw any definite conclusions on this, a task which is outside the scope of this work. However, some guide to the political sympathies of the boroughs can be obtained by studying a list made by Shaftesbury as the returns came in in the 1679 elections. Shaftesbury listed those M.P.s he thought would support him, those who favoured the Court, and a few he listed as doubtful.[5] There are a few inaccuracies in this list but, used in conjunction with the Exclusion Bill Division List,[6] a reasonably accurate indication of the political sympathies of borough M.P.s can be obtained. It must be remembered, however, that 'party' divisions were extremely fluid at this time, there being considerable divisions of opinion amongst Shaftesbury's own supporters. Many boroughs returned one M.P. of each persuasion. Shaftesbury considered that 302 members would support him (nearly 61 per cent), 158 (nearly 33½ per cent) were for the Court and 36 were doubtfuls, of whom about half voted against the Exclusion Bill. About the same percentage of M.P.s for each side were absent from the Exclusion vote. The

---

[3] *Life of Lord Keeper Guildford*, p. 115.

[4] Quoted in Burnet, *History of My Own Time*, iii, 1072.

[5] The list is published by J. R. Jones in *Bull. Inst. H.R.*, xxx, 232, 'Shaftesbury's Worthy Men', taken from the P.R.O. Shaftesbury Papers VIa/348.

[6] 'An Exclusion Division List', Browning and Milne, *Bull. Inst. H.R.*, xxiii, 205, taken from the list made by Roger Morrice which the writers consider more accurate than that in the P.R.O.

figures for the Exclusion division showed 207 for, 128 against and 174 absent. Eighty per cent of those M.P.s supporting the Bill were again returned at the election for the same constituencies in 1680, whereas only 55 per cent of those against the Bill were so returned. These figures indicate the great strength of the Whig cause between 1679 and 1681. It is true that after 1681 the Whig cause declined and many previously Whig boroughs petitioned the King 'abhorring' the Exclusion Bill and congratulating him on the dissolution of Parliament. These 'abhorrers' were influenced by the Rye House Plot, the fear of Civil War and the growing realisation that the Court was gaining in strength, especially after the *Quo Warranto* was issued against the City of London in December 1681. It would be difficult to say whether the electors in these boroughs had sincerely changed their political opinions, but it was clear that the King could not safely rely on them. Permanent control could only be obtained by altering the borough constitutions.[7]

However, the Court does not seem to have confined its attention to 'Whig' boroughs. Those boroughs to whom new charters were granted from 1681 until March and April 1685 when the Elections were held, returned, in 1679 elections, about 79 members broadly in sympathy with Shaftesbury and the Exclusion Bill and 53 members in sympathy with the Court's cause. This represents a percentage of 59 per cent Whig and 41 per cent Tory whereas the total percentage of M.P.s returned in 1689 was 61 per cent Whig and 33½ per cent Tory. Thus, proportionately, a slightly higher percentage of boroughs with some pro-Court sympathies were attacked. It is at least clear that Tory boroughs were not exempt. This is not surprising as the officers of Tory boroughs were more likely to surrender as soon as, or before, being required to do so in order to please the King and ensure that they were named as officers in the new charters. Whig boroughs, whose officers were likely to lose their positions on surrender, would naturally use delaying tactics on being

---

[7] For example, Wiltshire boroughs, previously strongly Whig, joined the ranks of the abhorrers. Victoria County Histories, *Wiltshire*, v, pp. 162 ff.

required to surrender. An example is York where the Whig magnates, in order to prevent surrender of the charter offered to elect a Tory Lord Mayor, return Tory members at the next election and replace a High Steward who had incurred the Court's disapproval by appointing the Duke of York or Halifax. This offer was refused, as the King did not feel any need to be conciliatory. He was in a strong position with the London decision behind him.[8] Similarly in Bristol after a *quo warranto* was issued against the charter, the city addressed the King saying that they had taken the advice of the Duke of Beaufort in electing a mayor and sheriffs to guarantee their loyalty. The King still required the City to surrender.[9] In Poole on being issued with a *quo warranto* in November 1683 the corporation petitioned the King congratulating him on his escape from the Rye House Plot and promised to elect loyal officers. However, they would not surrender and a judgement of seizure was entered against them and no new charter was granted until 1688.

Had the Court followed any plan in obtaining surrenders, it might also be imagined that it would concentrate on certain 'key' counties. Certain counties returned a large number of M.P.s, disproportionate to their size and population.[10] Cornwall, Devon, Dorset and Wiltshire in the South-West returned a total of 124 M.P.s, about a quarter of the House of Commons. In the South-East, Kent, Sussex, Surrey, Hampshire, Berkshire and the Cinque Ports returned 95 M.P.s, one-fifth of the Commons. In the North only Yorkshire returned a large number of members, and it of course is a large county. The Crown's attack was directed against these counties but no more than against other counties. The attack on the boroughs was launched against the whole of the country from the beginning and these over-represented boroughs were certainly not singled out for immediate or special attention, even though a very large part of the support for the Exclusion Bill came from these counties. Boroughs in Cornwall were

[8] Foxcroft, *Halifax*, p. 175.
[9] *Bristol Charters* 1509–1899, pp. 43 ff., ed. R. C. Latham, Bristol Record Soc., xii.
[10] *Royal Hist. Soc. Trans.* xxx, 29, Browning.

systematically attacked by the Earl of Bath, most Devon boroughs lost their charters and many in Yorkshire were induced to surrender by Judge Jeffreys. However, in Dorset only 4 of the 9 boroughs received new charters; in the strongly Whig Wiltshire[11] 7 out of 15 boroughs received new charters; in Surrey, again strongly Whig, only 1 out of 6 boroughs was re-incorporated; in Sussex 1 of 9 boroughs received a new charter.

A total of 67 English parliamentary boroughs did not lose their charters within this period (1681–8).[12] In 1679 these boroughs returned about 89 members supporting Shaftesbury and about 45 supporting the Court. It cannot be said that 'loyal' boroughs only were exempt. What other reasons were there for leaving these 67 boroughs alone? Again only a detailed study of the history of each borough at this time would lead to any unassailable conclusions. However, it is clear from the list that few large or important towns or cities are included. Of the two cities in the list Durham was under the patronage of the Bishop, who incorporated it, and was firmly pro-Court, and Stafford was also Tory. Some of the boroughs who did not receive new charters were 'rotten', easily controlled by other means and not meriting the trouble and expense of a new charter,[13] though it is true that some 'rotten' boroughs did receive new charters, such as Wootton Basset in Wiltshire and many in Cornwall. The franchise in many of these boroughs rested on burgage tenure and was, therefore, easily controlled by the local landowner.[14] Granting new charters to such boroughs would not necessarily increase the Crown's control over the voters. The Crown concentrated largely on those boroughs in which the franchise vested in the Corporation, or in freemen created by the corporation, or where, by

[11] Victoria County Histories, *Wiltshire*, v, 162 ff. Shaftesbury was of course a local man.

[12] For list see Appendix B.

[13] E.g. Michael, Petersfield, Lymington, Gatton.

[14] E.g. Ashbourton, Belraston, Horsham, Midhurst, Bletchingley, East Grinstead, Downton, Heytesbury, Cricklade, Great Bedwin, Ludgershall, Old Sarum, Thirsk, Haselmere, Webley, Petersfield, Whitchurch, Corfe Castle, Westbury, Droitwich.

virtue of their ownership of land or control of poor relief and other alms,[15] the corporations controlled the franchise.

Thus the conclusion appears to be that the attack on the corporations did not proceed in accordance with any plan as to order of precedence. Nor was the desire to control Parliament the sole consideration. Of the total of 240 new charters granted between 1681 and 1688, 82 were granted, on surrender or forfeiture, to boroughs which had no right to return M.P.s and to other companies, such as trading companies and livery companies. Membership of a London Livery Company conferred membership of the city corporation and the right to elect M.P.s and officers. Twenty such livery companies lost their charters. However, the motive in remodelling the remaining 62 corporations must have been solely a desire to control their internal affairs, and to reward loyal friends of the King by appointing them to offices.

Many of these surrenders were not enrolled, despite the fact that the new charters were issued, and thus they were legally ineffective, though of course they were not challenged in the Courts until after the Revolution. In some cases it was necessary actually to start *quo warranto* proceedings, but none were properly defended. Chester initially resolved to defend itself, but eventually judgement was entered for non-appearance and a new charter was granted.[16] Similarly Oxford resolved to defend a *quo warranto*, but then defaulted. The grounds for these *quo warrantos* were often trivial. For instance, the basis of one against Bristol was that they had chosen in various years 49, 51, and 53 officers, when they should have chosen 43 every year.[17] Bristol surrendered under this threat. The corporations were generally too poor to defend themselves,[18] and it was thought by many that the King meant to forfeit what revenue they had, though in fact the King

[15] In many boroughs householders receiving alms etc. forfeited the right to vote.

[16] Which caused extensive litigation after the Revolution, see *R.* v. *Amery* (1786) 2 T.R.

[17] Merewether and Stephens, op. cit., iii, 1795.

[18] See above, pp. 2–4.

was only interested in controlling the personnel. The interesting case of *Att-Gen. v. Lord Gower*[19] provides an example of the efforts of one corporation to protect their property from the King. Newcastle had been prevailed upon to surrender its charter in 1684 but, before dispatching the Mayor to London to accomplish the surrender, the Common Council agreed to make a lease of all the corporation property for one thousand years to trustees, in trust to permit the Corporation to use the rents and profits for the benefit of the poor. In this case the lease was held invalid as it had never been acted upon and was made in contemplation of an event which never occurred, namely the seizure of the Corporation property by the King.

However, just as many of the surrenders had not been enrolled, so many of the judgements of seizure were not entered on the Court Record, despite the grant of new charters. This is made clear by James II's Proclamation of 7 October 1688, which restored those corporations whose surrenders were not enrolled, or whose judgements of seizure had not been recorded, to their ancient charters.[20] The Proclamation admitted that these surrenders and judgements were not legally effective. It is clear that, after the London Case was won, the Crown abandoned any attempt to appear to be acting legally. This is also shown by the fact that most of the new charters directly altered the Parliamentary franchise, which could not legally be altered by the King alone.[21] The franchise was restricted to the members of the corporations, whose appointment and dismissal was controlled by the Crown.

The form of the new borough charters has already been

[19] (1740) Mod. 224.
[20] *London Gazette*, Oct. 15, 1688. The following surrenders were enrolled: Thetford, Nottingham, Bridgewater, Ludlow, Beverley, Tewkesbury, Exeter, Doncaster, Colchester, Winchester, Launceston, Liskeard, Plympton, Tregony, Plymouth, Dunwich, St Ives, Fowey, East Looe, Camelford, West Looe, Tintagel, Penryn, Truro, Bodmyn, Hadleigh, Lostwythell and Saltash.
The following judgements were entered: London, Chester, Calne, St Ives, Pool, York, Thaxted, Laughon and Malmesbury.
[21] Thetford Charter, above, p. 82. See also below, pp. 107 ff.

mentioned.[22] Their effect was to give the King control over the officers and Parliamentary franchise; but he did not desire or obtain control over their property as was feared. In fact extra privileges and sources of income were often granted. Bristol's new charter gave them three corn and grain markets, three wool markets and five horse fairs, but on the other hand all official appointments needed Royal approval and the officials could be also removed by the Crown. An interesting and typical example of the type of new charter granted is that of Portsmouth in 1682.[23] The Charter created Portsmouth a body corporate and named the First Mayor and twelve Aldermen. The body corporate was to consist of them and the Burgesses, who were also named in the charter. Burgesses thus named included the Duke of York, Lord Finch, Lord Noell, Earl Conway, Secretary of State Jenkins, Francis North, Edmund Saunders and many other Court officials. The object obviously was to exclude the inhabitants of the town from being Burgesses, and place the power and the Parliamentary franchise in a select, safely Royalist body. All the officers of the corporation were to be at the appointment of the Mayor, Aldermen and Burgesses and the King was given the power to remove any of them. Certain additional privileges were granted, such as the 'assize of bread', fines, felon's goods and extra markets and fairs. The Burgesses and inhabitants were to be quit of toll and not compellable to pay lighthouse duties.

As has been noted, the boroughs were not the only corporations to lose their charters. All the London Livery Companies, some trading companies and Colleges also lost theirs. Many of the chief Livery Companies were served with *quo warrantos* and they promptly asked the King what he wished of them.[24] He replied frankly that he had no wish to deprive them of their privileges or property, but only to have some control over their governing bodies. The forms of surrender and regrant were almost the same for all companies, making the King's approval necessary to the

[22] Above, pp. 3–4.
[23] Merewether and Stephens, op. cit., iii, 1718.
[24] Luttrell, *A Brief Historical Relation of State Affairs*, i, 304–5.

appointment of Wardens and Clerks, and giving him the power to remove them.[25] The Merchant Taylors made a particularly obsequious surrender, presenting a humble address of thanks for the new charter, and giving Sir George Jeffreys (who was said to be the virtual ruler of London at that time)[26] a present of plate for which each Assistant of the Society contributed fifty shillings.[27] The Drapers' Company invited Jeffreys to a Stewards' Dinner and made him a guest at all their public dinners.[28] Massachusetts also lost its charter in 1684, a *scire facias* being issued on the grounds (among others) that Massachusetts had 'incorporated' Harvard College, which was contrary to the Royal Prerogative as only the Crown can bestow incorporation.[29] The Bermudas Company also lost its charter on a *quo warranto*.

This 'reform' of the corporations had the desired result and the first and only Parliament called by James II in 1685 was completely subservient to the Royal interest. 'Everything was granted with such profusion that the House was more ready to give than the King to ask.'[30] James himself said that 'there were not above forty members, but such as he wished for'.[31]

Of the 513 M.P.s, 200 were directly dependent on the King for their livelihood. Four hundred of the members were new to the House of Commons.[32] Triumphant though the Court was, the result had not been confidently expected and great effort was made to organise an electioneering campaign. The Court could not be confident that the regulation of the corporations would carry the election for them as by that time only 77 parliamentary boroughs had received their new charters. The election campaign was organised by Sunderland for the King and, even though the

[25] Herbert, W., *History of the Twelve Great Livery Companies*, i, 218 (London, 1837).

[26] See, for an example, Rep. 90 f. 84, Reresby, *Memoirs*, p. 308.

[27] ibid., p. 215.

[28] Johnson, A. H., *History of the Drapers Company* (Oxford, 1914–22), p. 298.

[29] 3 *Select Essays in Anglo-American Local History* (1907–09), p. 241. *Cal.S.P.Dom.* 1684, p. 51.

[30] Burnet, op. cit., iii, 13.

[31] Quoted in Merewether and Stephens, op. cit., iii, 1817.

[32] *The Century of Revolution*, J. E. C. Hill (Edinburgh, 1961), p. 234.

Whigs were by this time completely unorganised there were some
hotly contested elections.[33] However, even this Parliament was
not prepared to acquiesce quietly to everything the King proposed, and after it had made a gentle protest against the dispensing
of the Test Act and the appointment of Roman Catholics to
public offices, James dismissed it. In 1687, in preparation for an
election, James appointed 'regulators' to inspect the corporations
and reform them, obtaining surrenders where other reforms were
impossible. They also examined the qualifications of electors. In
order to ensure that only the well affected were nominated as
candidates or permitted to become electors, Lord Lieutenants
and judges were required to ask the leading citizens three questions,
(1) would they support the repeal of the penal laws and the Test
Acts, (2) would they vote for a candidate who would support
such repeal, and (3) would they support a declaration of liberty
of conscience and be friendly to all persons of all persuasions?
The answers revealed little support for James and many of the
returns were inaccurate.[34] The Regulators were 'a sort of motley
council made up of Catholics and Presbyterians'.[35] James's
attempt to gain the dissenters as allies was based on the fact that
the repeal of the Test Act and the Penal Laws favoured them as
well as the Roman Catholics. The Regulators appointed many
dissenters (there not being a sufficient number of Catholics to fill
posts) to positions in corporations in the place of high Tories who
were in favour of retaining Penal Laws. Sixty-seven former
Whig M.P.s who had voted for exclusion were listed as suitable
to be appointed as parliamentary candidates or Justices of the
Peace. Whigs who had been replaced by Tories in the early part of
the campaign against Corporations now found themselves replacing those Tories. In Nottingham Whigs who had been fined
for rioting against the surrender of the charter in 1682 were now
installed in the again remodelled corporation.[36] This intensive

[33] See the account of this election by George, *R. Hist. Soc. Trans.*, xix (1936),
167.
[34] 'James II's Whig Collaborators', J. R. Jones, *Hist. Journal*, iii, 1 (1960), 65.
[35] Hallam, H. *The Constitutional History of England* (London, 1872), iii, 74.
[36] *Hist. Journal*, iii, 1 (1960), 65.

campaigning was accompanied in 1687/8 by a further effort against the charters. The control gained over the corporations in the new charters was not effective enough. The new charters gave the Crown the right only to remove certain officers. The charters issued in 1688 also gave the Crown the right to fill any vacancy that occurred on removal, within twenty days. The officers were exempted from taking oaths and tests, and the appointment of certain officials, such as town clerks and recorders, required Royal approval before they were permitted to function. The franchise was restricted to the corporation. Twenty-four boroughs which had already been re-incorporated since 1681 were further re-modelled in 1688.[37] *Quo warrantos* were used to induce surrenders and judgements by default recorded. The King also used the powers of removal that he already had to such an extent that many considered that the corporations, being bereft of almost all their officers, were *de facto* dissolved and therefore the inhabitants petitioned for new charters.[38] James had three weapons with which to attack the corporations; he could use the powers of removal given in all charters granted since 1681, he could obtain judgement on a *quo warranto* for abuser, and he could bring pressures on the corporations to make them surrender. He seemed to use all three at once in some cases. Mr George in his article in the *English Historical Review* notes that a *quo warranto* was issued against Kingston which resulted in surrender but even so, all the officers of the corporation were removed by order in council, which was considered to dissolve the corporation. Again Nottingham voted to surrender after a *quo warranto* had been issued in May 1688 but nevertheless judgement and a writ of seizure were issued in July. Winchester had surrendered in 1684 but had never received a new charter. However, the Crown, having presumably forgotten this, again requested surrender in 1688. The surrender was then enrolled.

[37] They were Buckingham, Chester, Barnstaple, Tiverton, Calne, Ipswich, Kingston upon Hull, Nottingham, Wells, Oxford, Poole, Lynn Regis, Bridport, Colchester, Grimsby, Newcastle upon Tyne, Evesham, Salisbury, Leicester, Boston, Grantham, Norwich, Brackley, Morpeth.

[38] For details see George, 'Charters Granted to Parliamentary Corporations in 1688', *E.H.R.*, lv (1940), 47.

Judgement on a *quo warranto* against this non-existent corporation was entered in the King's Bench and a writ of seizure issued. Also, to make quite sure that the Winchester corporation would not rise from the dead, all the corporation's officials were removed by order in council. These are plainly the activities of desperate men. As can be imagined, the alliance of Catholics and dissenters was incongruous and uneasy, the latter being, traditionally, fanatical anti-Papists, remembering the recent oppressions they had suffered. It was not difficult for the Anglicans to alienate them with promises of tolerance. Thus James had recklessly thrown away the support of the Tories by his promotion of the Catholics and had also lost the support, which had in any case never been very wholehearted, of the dissenters. Despite all his measures regulating corporations Sunderland advised James not to call another Parliament. After the trial of the Seven Bishops and the birth of an heir, James's support waned still further.

The extent to which Royal interference in the corporations was resented is shown by the fact that one of James's first acts, on hearing of the invitation extended to the Prince of Orange, was to restore to their ancient constitutions those corporations whose surrenders had not been enrolled or who had not had judgements entered against them. Separate Proclamations restored the charter to the City of London, Winchester, Doncaster and Poole but it was too late to regain the support of either the City or the Country and William of Orange became King.

A Bill to restore the corporations to their position before the events of Charles II's and James II's reigns was introduced into the Convention Parliament and passed the Commons. However, before it could get through the Lords, Parliament was dissolved and the Bill struck out. Thus the hasty Proclamation of James II remained the only measure upon which most of the corporations could rely to revive their old charters. The situation became chaotic, some corporations having acted on the Proclamation and others having ignored it. There resulted a great many applications for new charters, and a considerable amount of litigation. Where a Corporation's surrender had not been enrolled and it had subsequently accepted and acted upon the Proclamation then the old charter was held to be revived and all subsequent charters void.[39] However, some corporations continued to act under the charters granted to them by Charles or James, even though their surrenders had not been enrolled. For instance, it was not until 1710 that the Burgesses of Bristol refused to act under their charter of 1684, granted after an unenrolled surrender, and were granted a new charter by Anne.[40] Colchester's surrender had been enrolled and, therefore, did not come within the scope of the Proclamation. In 1689 the persons who should have elected officers under the Charter of James II refused to act, to the detriment of the peace of the town. William bade them continue to operate under that charter until he had time to restore the corporations their ancient privileges[41] (which he did not do). They continued under this charter until 1740 when a judgement of ouster was recorded against the mayor and aldermen. From 1740 no officers were elected or appointed until a new charter was granted in 1763. Bewdley, in the same position as Colchester, continued to act under its James II Charter until 1832 (when the Reform Act was passed) despite the fact that in 1710 a Committee of the House of Commons had declared the charter illegal as it interfered with the franchise.[42]

Although it has been accepted since 1766, when *Colchester v. Seaber* was decided, that charters could be both forfeited and surrendered, these measures have rarely again been used against borough corporations. There are a few cases, brought generally by individuals, of mayors and other officers being ousted of their positions by *quo warranto* because of defects in the elections. After 1688 they were virtually free of all central control, and many of the fears, expressed by Sawyer and others, that corrupt and virtually unassailable pockets of power would establish themselves in fact came true.[43] By the Statute of 9 Anne c.20 (1710), an

---

[39] *Newling* v. *Francis*, (1789) 3 T.R. 189.
[40] Mereweather and Stephens, op. cit., iii, 1953.
[41] *Cal.S.P.Dom.* 1689/90, p. 225.   [42] Grant, *Law of Corporations*, p. 45.
[43] Thompson, *Constitutional History of England*, p. 455.

information against a corporation to question their right to be a corporation could only be brought by the Attorney-General. The system of local government became corrupt and inefficient and abuses grew for which there was no effective statutory remedy. The excesses of the Stuart period made any interference into the affairs of the boroughs a politically dangerous act. The Royal Commission whose findings prompted the Municipal Corporations Act 1835 found local Courts and Magistrates corrupt, revenues misapplied, property improperly alienated and statutory duties neglected. But few writs of *scire facias* or *quo warranto* were issued to remedy these defects.[44] The Commission reported that the affairs of the boroughs were managed with the utmost secrecy, many of the members being bound by oath. The people of the boroughs could not know what regulations had been passed, or whether the charters had been violated save by an expensive and troublesome *mandamus* or *quo warranto*.[45]

[44] See Glover, *Law of Municipal Corporations* (1841), Introduction, p. xli; the only example I have found of a *scire facias* to annul a charter of incorporation after 1688 is that of *R. v. Eastern Archipelago Co.* (1853) 2 E. & B. 856.

[45] Royal Commission into Municipal Corporations, 1835, para. 79.

CHAPTER VII

The Legal Validity of the Surrenders

THE QUESTION of whether a corporation could legally surrender its charter was not strictly relevant to the issues in the London Case, but it was discussed. The contention that a corporation could not surrender its charter arose inevitably from the City's concept of the powers of a corporation. A corporation could validly perform only those activities authorised by its charter, and no existing charter authorised the Common Council, or anyone else, to surrender it. On the contrary, the members of the Common Council had to take oaths that they would preserve the liberties of the City.[1] Two cases were cited by the City to support their contention: the *Dean and Chapter of Norwich's Case*,[2] and *Hayward* v. *Fulcher*[3] (which concerned the same surrender). The Dean and Chapter of Norwich surrendered their church and all their franchises and heriditaments, and this was accepted by the King, who granted a new corporation to them. It was held that this was not a good surrender of the body politic, and the old corporation remained. There is also the case of the *Dean and Chapter of Wells*,[4] who attempted to surrender their corporation. This was held ineffective without an Act of Parliament. The King, said Treby, cannot dissolve a corporation. In the many statutes concerning the dissolution of the monasteries by Henry VIII[5] the words 'surrendered and forfeited' were used, but these did not refer to the actual corporation, but merely to its lands and franchises.[6] This is tacitly recognised in the Statute concerning the Knights of St John at Jerusalem,[7] where it is provided that the corporation of St John shall be dissolved and

---

[1] Pollexfen, *S.T.*, viii, 1225. [2] (1590) 3 Coke 73; 2 Anderson 120.
[3] (1628) Palmer 491; Jones 166. [4] (1568) Dyer 273 (*Walrond* v. *Pollard*).
[5] For example, 27 Hen. 8; 30 Hen. 8, c. 13. [6] Treby, *S.T.*, viii, 1109.
[7] 32 Hen. 8, c. 24.

the King have their lands. The fact that the statute directly enacts that they shall be dissolved (which the former statutes did not do), shows that the surrender of their lands and their vesting in the King did not in fact dissolve the corporation. Many of the Abbots in Henry VIII's time may have thought that their corporations were dissolved, and so they might have been in fact, but in law they continued.[8] Treby could find only one case against him, and that is *Archbishop of Dublin* v. *Bruerton*,[9] where a Dean and Chapter surrendered and this was held to dissolve the corporation. Treby had certain objections to the authority of this case. First, the validity of the surrender was not the point at issue. Second, it was a private, extra-judicial opinion of five judges only, the case having been sent by the Irish Judges to the English because they had doubts on the point. Third, the case was wrongly decided because, in any case, the Dean and Chapter could not surrender without the consent of the Bishop. Fourth, Treby casts doubt on the authenticity of Dyer's report, stating Coke's opinion that the surrender was by act of Parliament or it would have been invalid. Sawyer did not attempt to deal with the question of surrender in detail because it was not in issue and, significantly, 'because the point may come judicially into debate, some dislike having been taken to surrenders lately made'.[10] Concerning the *Norwich Case* and *Hayward* v. *Fulcher*, Sawyer contends that it was admitted throughout the latter case that a corporation could be surrendered, the question being whether the Dean and Chapter could surrender without the concurrence of the Bishop. It is true that Whitlock J. considered that for a corporation to surrender would be a *felo de se*, and against nature, but this was denied by Jones who says that a Dean and Chapter may be dissolved by cesser or where all the members die. Jones nevertheless agreed that the surrender in issue did not in fact dissolve the corporation, because of the non-concurrence of the Bishop. When it was stated that the King can create but not dissolve a corporation all that was meant was that he could not dissolve it without reason, and due process of law.

[8] Palmer 495.   [9] (1569) Dyer 282.   [10] Sawyer, *S.T.*, viii, 1163.

It was not until after 1688 that the surrenders under Charles II and James II came up for judicial review. In 1689 a bill was introduced into the Commons to restore the corporations to their ancient privileges, the first section of which recited that the surrenders of corporations 'were and are illegal and void'. The Lords took the advice of the Judges[11] on this point and decided to strike out this phrase, despite the fact that six of the ten judges denied that a corporation could surrender. Only one, Holt C. J. was definitely of the opinion that corporations could surrender, the other three being uncertain but inclined to agree with Holt. Holt maintained that a corporation was a franchise, derived from the Crown and could be dissolved by surrender. His authorities were *Walrond* v. *Pollard*,[12] concerning the surrender of the Deanery of Wells, which he admitted had the confirmation of an Act, and *Archbishop of Dublin* v. *Bruerton*,[13] where the Judges certified that a corporation could be surrendered and thus dissolved. Holt considered that the *Norwich Case* was against him but 'that a corporation is dissoluble all the books say'. Pollexfen C. J. held the same view as when he appeared for the City, namely that a corporation may be dissolved by death or cessation, but not by choosing, any more than can a natural person surrender his capacity. Corporations are created to govern towns and for them to surrender their charters would be a *felo de se*. He considers the *Norwich Case* strong authority for this view. Dolben J. (who received his *quietus* in 1683 because, it was rumoured, he was not expected to support the King in the London Case)[14] states that a corporation cannot surrender or forfeit, but does not examine any authorities. Lechmere B., Rokeby J., Ventris J., and Turton J., all deny for various reasons that a corporation can surrender, especially because it would be breaking the trust of a corporation to do so, and cause many inconveniences. Lechmere stresses that corporations who send members to Parliament cannot surrender. Gregory B., and Eyre J., are doubtful but inclined to favour the

---

[11] See *H.M.C. 12th Report*, part VI, p. 429.
[12] (1568) Dyer 273.   [13] (1569) Dyer 282.
[14] Luttrell, *A Brief Historical Relation of State Affairs*, i, 255.

capacity to surrender. Eyre makes the point that where a corporation surrenders it reverts to its Borough status, the implication being that the surrender will not interfere with the Parliamentary franchise, as Lechmere implied.[15] The Lord Chief Baron gave an interesting opinion which has never been adopted. Some corporations, he said, may surrender, but others not. 'It seems to me rational that where for private ends a corporation is granted, they may[16] surrender'. However, where a charter is granted for public purposes, it may not be surrendered. Though the charter is 'granted to a small town, it is not theirs, it is the whole Kingdom's. The interest of all the people of England is concerned and that, it is clear, cannot be surrendered'. But he does not give any authorities to support this contention, however 'clear' he may consider the point to be.[17]

The Corporations' Restoration Bill was struck out because of the dissolution of the Convention Parliament in January 1690, but not before a Protest had been registered by certain Lords against the deletion of the words 'illegal and void' in the first section.[18] The grounds were that the only two examples of surrenders were the *Wells Case* and the *Dublin Case*; the former required an Act of Parliament to make the surrender valid, and the latter was denied to be law in *Hayward* v. *Fulcher*. The Protest also quoted the case of the Corporation of Newbury which surrendered to Henry V, where the House of Commons called upon them to send members notwithstanding the surrender.[19] Apparently the Lords, in deciding to strike out the words 'illegal and void', were

---

[15] See further on this point p. 107 below.

[16] This is printed as 'may not' in the 12th Report, but must be a misprint as it makes nonsense of the passage.

[17] It would seem that this idea was in fact adopted by the Municipal Corporations Act 1835. Grant is of the opinion that corporations governed by this Act cannot surrender: 'it appears evident from the tone of the Municipal Corporations Act that the Legislature intended to impose permanent and indefeasible duties on the bodies to which it applied,' *Law of Corporations*, p. 46. Other chartered corporations may still surrender, he considers.

[18] Protests of the Lords, January 23, 1690. *H.C. Journals*.

[19] But, as was pointed out by Merewether and Stephens, the right to send M.P.s does not depend on being incorporated, but on having borough status.

influenced by the surrenders of the abbeys under Henry VIII. Burnet says that 'there was little doubt at the passing of the Act' and
that the Convention Parliament was dissolved to avoid it, but this
appears unlikely, especially as the first clause had been defeated by
51 to 43 votes (and not passed by one vote as Burnet alleges).[20]

A number of cases arose from the surrenders under Charles II
and James II. Many of the surrenders were not in fact enrolled,
even though new charters were issued. The Courts were unani-
mous in deciding that a surrender that was not enrolled was void,
and therefore a charter granted after a void surrender was also
void.[21] But these surrenders were in any case subject to James II's
Proclamation in 1688[22] restoring all corporations whose surrenders
were not enrolled, or whose charters were forfeited by judgements
which were not entered, to their ancient rights and privileges. In
Newling v. *Francis*[23] it was held that if the proclamation had been
accepted, it operated as a grant of revival of the old charters and
extinguished such new charters as were granted by the King after
the surrender. It was also clear that a corporation is not dissolved
by surrendering all its property to the King, at least where it still
has some function to perform. In *R.* v. *Mayor of London*,[24] Holt
maintained that the surrender by a town of all its rights and
privileges did not necessarily dissolve the corporation as it still
had some duties to perform, namely the government of the town.
The effect of surrenders that were enrolled gave rise to difficulties.
In *Piper* v. *Dennis*,[25] a *quo warranto* had been brought against the
town of Liskeard; it surrendered, the surrender was enrolled, and a
new charter granted by James II. It was held that the new charter,
being in consideration of a void surrender, was also void. No
further details are given in the report. In *R.* v. *Grey*[26] three of the
four judges were of the opinion that surrender did not dissolve

---

[20] Burnet, *History of My Own Time*, iv, 69.

[21] *Butler* v. *Palmer* (1700) 1 Salk. 191 (Concerning the surrender of Dartmouth;
Held: void for non enrollment.) *R.* v. *Osborne* (1803) 4 East 327 (Concerning the
surrender of Kingston upon Hull; Held: void for non enrollment).

[22] *London Gazette*, Oct. 15th–18th, 1688.

[23] (1789) 3 T.R. 189.   [24] (1692) 12 Mod., at p. 19 (*Sir James Smith's Case*).
[25] Holt 170.   [26] (1725) 8 Mod. 358.

the corporation, the authorities relied on being the same as those quoted above, and stress being laid on the fact that the surrenders of the abbeys under Henry VIII did not dissolve them. But this case was adjourned and judgement does not seem ever to have been given. By 1766 it was accepted by Lord Mansfield in the *Mayor of Colchester* v. *Seaber*[27] that a corporation could be dissolved by surrender and that if this happens all the land of the corporation reverts to the grantor, and its goods and chattels go to the Crown. In *R. v. Amery*[28] the point was not in issue, but the Crown, who eventually won the case, submitted that a corporation could not surrender itself, citing the *Norwich Case* and *R. v. Grey*. The arguments of the Crown Counsel in this case are taken straight from Treby's in the London Case. The Defence maintained that by that time it had long been considered that a corporation could be dissolved and cited the case of *Colchester* v. *Seaber*.

Blackstone, writing in 1765, states categorically that corporations may be dissolved by surrender, 'which is a kind of suicide', without giving any authorities or even indicating that the point was controversial.[29] Kyd, in his 'Law of Corporations' 1793-4, examines the question more thoughtfully.[30] He recognises that in *R. v. Amery* and *R. v. Grey* it was maintained that corporations could not be surrendered and that the cases quoted by the Crown in favour of dissolution by surrender in the London Case are open to valid objections. However he is of the opinion that corporations can be dissolved by surrender. (He ridicules Treby's contention that corporations are immortal.) There is no 'metaphysical' difficulty to prevent surrender. A corporation, writes Kyd, can dissolve itself in much the same way as a person can kill himself. Whether it should be allowed to do so is a political point, but it does not seem to be established that such a surrender is illegal. Therefore, although there are no strong authorities providing that a corporation may surrender, it can be assumed in the absence

---

[27] (1766) 3 Burr. 1866. He also held, however, that a new charter could revive the old corporation.
[28] (1786) 2 T.R. 515; Reverses 4 T.R. 122.
[29] Blackstone, *Commentaries*, i, 484 ff.   [30] Kyd, *Law of Corporations*, ii, 465 ff.

of any provision forbidding it, that it is legal, as there is nothing
inherent in the nature of a corporation to prevent it. In any case,
Kyd points out, it would be 'impossible to prevent the natural
effect of a surrender actually made'.[31] It is accepted that where a
corporation entirely ceases to function and is incapable of
functioning, as where all the members die, it is dissolved. A
completed surrender would have this very effect. Such a surrender,
if made without the authority of the rest of the corporation,
would be a breach of trust by the officers,

but unless the [whole corporation] had, by the original constitution of
the corporation, the power of supplying the place of the [officers] by
an election from among themselves, I do not see how the effect of a
complete destruction of the corporate existence could be prevented.[32]

It will be noted that here Kyd implies that if the surrender were
with the authority of the rest of the corporation, then it would not
be even a breach of trust. According to the doctrine of *ultra vires*,
which was not, of course, fully elaborated until the mid-nineteenth
century, such an act, not being within the constitution of the
corporation, would be void. Whether or not the doctrine of
ultra vires did or does apply to chartered corporations had been
disputed, but it seems probable that it did.[33] Even so Kyd's point
remains. The surrender being *ultra vires* the charter would be
legally void, but the surrender would have the effect of depriving
the corporation of an integral part and prevent the corporation
from functioning. Thus the law would not be able to prevent the
corporation's dissolution. However, this assumes that a corporation which cannot operate because all its members are dead or
gone is dissolved. The strict application of the fiction theory
would not have this result as, according to that theory, the
existence of the corporation is not dependent on the individual
existence of its members. Gower quotes a modern case where,
during the Second World War, all the members of a private company were killed by a bomb whilst in general meeting, but the

[31] Kyd, op. cit., ii, 466.   [32] ibid.
[33] See above, p. 75.

company nevertheless survived.[34] But, whatever the position today, it seems clear that in the seventeenth and eighteenth centuries at least this was not the law and Treby, a clear supporter of the fiction theory, had no difficulty in recognising that a corporation is dissolved where all the members are dead.[35] In Roll's Abridgement f.514 it is stated that where a large part of the corporation no longer exists and is incapable of being renewed, the corporation is dissolved. This was considered to be law when James II, in 'regulating' the corporations, dismissed most of the officers. The members considered the corporation thus dissolved and it was to obviate the inconvenience of this that the power to appoint officers, as well as to dismiss them, was given to the Crown in the charters granted in 1688.[36] Later it was held that the loss of its members merely suspends the existence of a corporation and does not dissolve it.[37]

Concerning the surrenders of the abbeys under Henry VIII, the validity of which Treby maintained was supported by Acts of Parliament, Kyd points out that the legal doubt which made these statutes necessary was not whether the monasteries could be dissolved by any surrender, but whether the terms of the surrenders actually made were sufficient to dissolve the corporations. This is implicit in the very manner in which Treby puts forward these statutes.[38] Kyd concludes that the rules adopted,

in all the cases which have occurred on this question seem to have been this: that when the effect of the surrender is to destroy the end for which the corporation or the corporate capacity was instituted, the corporation or corporate capacity is itself destroyed.

On this basis Kyd explains the *Norwich case*, the strongest authority

---

[34] Gower, L. C. B., *Modern Company Law*, 2nd ed. (1957), p. 71, n. 58.

[35] Treby, *S.T.*, viii, 1101, 1107; *R.* v. *Bewdley* (1712) 1 P.W. 207; *Banbury* (1716) 10 mod. 346; *Tregony* (1722) 8 mod. 127. During this time many corporations were held to be dissolved because they had neglected to elect a Mayor on the proper day and thus an integral part of the corporation had gone. The inconveniences resulting from this particular defect only were remedied by St. II Geo. C.4.

[36] See above, p. 92.

[37] *Colchester* v. *Seaber* (1766) 3 Burr. 1866; *R.* v. *Passmore* (1789) 3 T.R. 241.

[38] See above, p. 36.

quoted against surrender. The reason why the surrender of the church and all the possessions of the deanery did not dissolve the corporation was that the corporation still had a function to perform, for the bishopric remained and the Dean and Chapter were of the Bishop's council. The same applies to *Hayward* v. *Fulcher*, and this was the basis of the decision in *R.* v. *City of London* (1692).[39] However this does not surmount the objection that, from the language used, some of the judges in both these cases thought that a corporation could not surrender, Whitlock calling it a '*felo de se*, which is against nature'.

All writers since Kyd have assumed that it is possible for a corporation to surrender its charter, with the exception of corporations by prescription, which, having no charter to surrender, can only dissolve themselves by refuser to act.[40] Why this exception is maintained is difficult to fathom. The law assumes that a corporation by prescription once had a charter which was lost before the time of living memory. If the law can accept the existence of this fictional charter, it should have no difficulty in recognising the fictional surrender of the fictional charter. This exception was not raised by the City of London during the case or afterwards, when the question of surrender was directly in issue (London being a corporation by prescription). Many of the corporations which surrendered to Charles and James were corporations by prescription. In *Newling* v. *Francis*,[41] concerning the surrender by the corporation by prescription of Cambridge, it was not suggested that the surrender was ineffective for this reason.

There is one point made by the City which has not been satisfactorily answered in relation to the surrender of charters. If a corporation has only those powers given to it by its charter, how can it validly surrender that charter unless such a power is expressly given?[42] This question raises the wider issue of *ultra vires* in general. It has been thought that the *ultra vires* doctrine had

---

[39] (1692) Holt. 168. (See above, p. 59.)
[40] Grant, op. cit., p. 46; Holdsworth, *History of English Law*, ix, 65.
[41] (1789) 3 T.R. 189.   [42] See above, pp. 96–7.

never applied to chartered corporations; that, once set up, a chartered corporation had all the powers of a natural person; and that even if it did break any limitation on its powers made in its charter, the act was valid.[43]

If this statement of the law is correct, then there would be no objection to a corporation surrendering itself. This would, as Kyd says, be a kind of suicide and nowhere is the suicide of a corporation proscribed. However, there is strong evidence that in fact the *ultra vires* doctrine does apply to chartered corporations and that, even before this doctrine was evolved in its final form, it was never the law that chartered corporations had unlimited powers.[44] Thus, if a corporation acts outside the powers given it by its charter, those acts are void. Therefore, it cannot execute a valid deed of surrender. (It can of course achieve the same result as surrender simply by ceasing to function.)

Two other points arose from these surrenders. First, did they finally and irrevocably extinguish the corporation? One of the City's arguments in the London Case was that, by dissolving the corporation, all its ancient rights and privileges claimed by prescription would be extinguished, and many of them incapable of being regranted by the King. Also, all liability on debts owed to and by the City would be determined and any new corporation erected in its place would not be responsible for them, as it would have no privity with the old. Neither would it have any rights to the property of the old corporation, which, if realty, could revert to the donors. This would be the effect whether dissolution was by surrender, forfeiture or loss of an integral part. The desire to avoid these very inconvenient results was one reason why many lawyers denied that a corporation could be dissolved at all. Certain remarks of Lord Mansfield's in *Colchester* v. *Seaber*[45] were considered to support this view, but, as Kyd[46] points out,

[43] Though it would provide grounds for *quo warranto* or *scire facias* proceedings to dissolve the corporation.
[44] See Carden, 'Powers of Common Law Corporations', 26 *L.Q.R.* 320; Street, H. A., *Ultra Vires* (London, 1930).
[45] (1766) 3 Burr. 1866.
[46] Kyd, op. cit., ii, 516.

the real meaning of Lord Mansfield's words is that the rights and liabilities of the old corporations can be revived after its dissolution, if the King so desires, by the grant of a new charter to the old corporators. A grant of a charter to *new* corporators would not vest in them the rights and liabilities of the old corporation. This was held to be the law in *R.* v. *Passmore* (1789)[47] which concerned the dissolution of a corporation after the loss of an integral part. Kenyon J. pointed out the inconveniences which would result if the corporation was held to be finally dissolved and said that it should be considered to be dissolved for certain purposes, such as the issuing of a new charter. It did not follow, however, that because a corporation was dissolved for certain purposes, the King could not renovate it, and revive its old rights. Ashurst J., took a similar line, remarking that the difficulties had arisen from the equivocal use of the word dissolved, though it seems that the judges in this case used the word in a very equivocal fashion. The same decision had been arrived at in two earlier cases in 1681 and 1685, again arising from the grant of new charters by Charles II. In *Scarborough* v. *Butler*[48] a debt due to the old corporation was held to be due to the new corporation, even though it was incorporated under a different name. In *Haddock's Case*[49] a right to remove aldermen which had existed in the old charter held to exist under the new charter even though not mentioned in it. Thus for certain purposes, such as preventing the officers from acting, the corporation is dissolved, but for the purpose of granting a new charter to a recognisable body of men and reviving the old corporation, the corporation is still in existence. The corporation is really not dissolved at all but merely suspended. However, if the King does not issue a new charter, the corporation is then dissolved. How long the King can wait before making up his mind has never been considered. This rather illogical resolution of the difficulty has been accepted ever since.[50]

The second problem concerned the legality of both the

---

[47] 3 T.R. 241.   [48] (1685) 3 Less. 237.   [49] (1681) Raym. 439.
[50] Grant, op. cit., pp. 47, 302; Smith, H. A., *Law of Associations*, p. 108; Holdsworth, op. cit., ix, 63.

surrenders and the new charters from the constitutional point of view. It was established that the Parliamentary franchise could not be altered by the exercise of the Royal Prerogative. In his opinion on the surrenders given to the House of Lords, Lechmere considered that Parliamentary corporations could not surrender because this would alter the franchise.[51] However, it seems clear that where a borough corporation is deprived of its corporate capacity for any reason, it reverts to its Common Law Borough status and may continue to send M.P.s.[52] The right to send M.P.s does not depend on the fact of incorporation and existed long before boroughs were incorporated. Merewether and Stephens[53] quote the case of Taunton, which returned M.P.s from earliest times and yet was not incorporated until 1667. Bletchingly was found by a Committee of the House of Commons not incorporated, but had the Parliamentary Franchise. Thus there can be no objection on this ground to the surrenders.

However, just as Parliamentary borough status does not depend on the existence of a Royal charter, neither can the Crown confer that right by charter. Merewether and Stephens quote the cases of Queenborough and East Looe as being incorporated and authorised by charter to return M.P.s, and yet not actually returning them.[54] A Committee of the House of Commons in 1623[55] decided that a charter granted in 1553 to Chippenham could not alter the form or right of election. Most of the charters granted by Charles and James after 1683 altered the Parliamentary franchise in some way. They contained provisions by which corporators could be removed at the discretion of the Crown. This is also contrary to Magna Carta Ch.29 which provides that no man shall be disseised of his freehold (and a corporator has a freehold in his franchise) without due process of law. However, many of these charters were nevertheless accepted as valid by the Courts, on the

[51] Report of Committee of the House of Commons, 21 James I (Glanville 53); Merewether and Stephens, *History of the Boroughs and Municipal Corporations*, ii, 1109.
[52] Eyre, J. made this point, H.M.C. 12th Rep. above.
[53] op. cit., i, 165.   [54] op. cit., ii, 664, 1256.
[55] See note 51 above.

grounds that they have been accepted by the members of the corporations. Grant compared this with a statement of Lord Denman in *Rutter* v. *Chapman* (1841)[56] that 'acceptance, however complete, merely concludes the bargain with the Crown, and cannot remove any defects inherent in the charter which renders it invalid as a legal instrument. Indeed no question on the legal authority of a charter could ever arise, unless it were in fact accepted.' Grant says that these illegal charters were valid as against the corporators themselves, as they had accepted them, and all the cases decided on the basis of these charters were between the corporators and the Crown. But in *Rutter* v. *Chapman* the dispute was between the corporators and a third party, whose rights cannot be affected by the acceptance of an illegal charter. This would seem to be the most satisfactory explanation of the cases. There can be no doubt that most of the charters granted by Charles and James contained illegal provisions of this kind, but they were acted upon up to, and in some cases, long after, the Revolution, but were rarely challenged on this ground.

[56] 8 M. & W. at p. 116.

APPENDIX A

List of New Charters granted from 1680 to 1688 (September)

(From 12th Report, Historical Manuscripts Commission, Appendix, part 6, p. 289.)

(This list fails to include charters granted to Kingston on Hull and Morpeth in September 1688. See George, *E.H.R.* lv (1940), 47, and P.R.O. C 66/3311–3324.)

1681
    Thetford
1682–1682/3
    Hereford
    Tavistock
    Chard
    Portsmouth
    Derby
    Andover
    Nottingham
    Maidstone
    Norwich
1683–1683/4
    Saltash
    East India Co.
    Northampton
    Coventry
    Bridgewater
    Warwick
    Banbury
    Wells
    Higham Ferrers
    Newport
    Evesham

    Sandwich
1684–1684/5
    (*Under Charles II*)
    Shaftesbury
    Okehampton
    Stationers' Co.
    Bristol
    Plymouth
    Yarmouth
    Bury St Edmunds
    Bedford
    Richmond
    Tiverton Clothworkers
    Ipswich
    Lynn Regis
    Dartmouth
    Buckingham
    Scarborough
    Dover
    Oxford
    Totnes
    Wallingford
    Colchester
    Exeter

Barnstaple

Brewer's Co. (Exeter)

Canterbury

Macclesfield

Tiverton

Carlisle

Leicester

Lincoln

Holliston

Kirkby

Grocers' Co.

Lancaster

Mercers' Co.

Drapers' Co.

Plumbers' Co.

Saddlers' Co.

Lymne

South Moulton

Bath

Cambridge

Newcastle upon Tyne

Merchant Taylors' Co.

Fishmongers' Co.

Coopers' Co.

Preston

Leominster

Leathersellers' Co.

Apothecaries' Co.

Clothworkers' Co.

Chester

1684–1684/5

(*Under James II*)

Worcester

Birmingham Free School

Grantham

Tilers' & Bricklayers' Co.

Barbers' & Chirurgeons' Co.

Haberdashers' Co.

Hedon

Innholders' Co.

Newark

Dunwick

Wigan

Southwold

Bridport

Founders' Co.

Stamford

Wycombe

Orford

Chichester

Tregony

Grampound

Fowey

St Ives

East Looe

Calne

New Sarum

Boston

Beverley

Brewers' Co.

Shrewsbury

Chippenham

Blacksmiths' Co.

St Albans

Newcastle under Lyme

Devizes

Salters' Co.

Glaziers' Co.

Ironmongers' Co.

Pontefract

New Windsor

Sudbury

Neath

Ludlow

Doncaster

Bodmin

West Looe

Swansea

Malmesbury
Skinners' Co.
East Retford
1685–1685/6
    Vintners' Co.
    Cordwainers' Co.
    Penrhyn
    Liskeard
    Launceston
    Truro
    Harwich
    Liverpool
    Godmanchester
    Honiton
    Tintagel
    Camelford
    Plympton
    Bradninch
    Lostwithiel
    Cutlers' Co.
    Malchell
    Calne
    Scriveners' Co.
    Cooks' Co.
    Joiners' Co.
    Goldsmiths' Co.
    Bewdley
    Newbury
    Armourers' Co.
    Wilton
    Tallow Chandlers' Co.
    Stafford
    Trinity House
    Saffron Waldon
    York
    Appleby
    Kellington
    Kingston upon Thames
    Weavers' Co.

Butchers' Co.
Torrington
Poulterers' Co.
Hastings
Masons' Co.
Faversham
Romney
Girdlers' Co.
Waxchandlers' Co.
Carpenters' Co.
Dyers' Co.
Reading
East India Merchants
Abingdon
Brecknock
Carmarthen
Tewkesbury
Morpeth
Broaderers' Co.
Turners' Co.
Pewterers' Co.
Paintstainers' Co.
Maidenhead
Kingston on Hull
Upholders' Co.
Bakers' Co.
Guildford
1686–1686/7
    Curriers' Co.
    Fruiterers' Co.
    Huntingdon
    Litchfield
    White Paper Makers' Co.
    Berwick
    Grimsby
    Brackley
    Ripon
    Cardiff
    Maldon

Gravesend
Physicians' Co.
Jersey
Coach & Harness Makers' Co.
Free Fishermen of the Thames
Trinity House (Newcastle)
Merchant Taylors' Co.
   (Exeter)
Distillers' Co.
Exeter
1688–Oct 1688
   Totnes
   Poulterers' Co.
   Queenborough
   Newcastle upon Tyne
   Tamworth
   Hertford
   New Woodstock
   Nottingham
   Wells
   French Ministers
   Buckingham
   Evesham
   Tiverton
   Calne
   Salisbury
   Taunton
   Brackley
   Grimsby
   Chester
   Norwich
   Winchester

Colchester
Marlborough
Ipswich
Leicester
Grantham
Boston
Bridport
Lynn Regis
Cinque Ports
Oxford
Barnstaple
Bishops' Castle
Southampton
Pool
October 1688
   Restitution to the City of
   London of all franchise held
   before the Judgement on
   the Quo Warranto.
   Likewise to the Livery Com-
   panies of London.
   Likewise to the Mayor &
   Citizens of Chester.
November 1688
   Charters restored:
      Winchester
      Doncaster
      Grocers of London
      Vintners of London
      Drapers of London
December 1688
   Poole

APPENDIX B

English Parliamentary Boroughs whose Charters were not Remodelled

Buckinghamshire:
  Aylesbury
  Agmondesham
  Great Marlow
  Wendover
Cornwall:
  Micheal
  St Germans
  St Mawes
Cumberland:
  Cockermouth
Devon:
  Ashburton
  Dartmouth
  Belraston
Dorset:
  Dorchester
  Weymouth
  Melcombe Regis
  Wareham
  Corfe Castle
Durham City
Gloucestershire:
  Cirencester
Herefordshire:
  Weobly
Kent:
  Rochester
Lancashire:
  Clithero

Middlesex:
  Westminster
Norfolk:
  Castlerising
Northamptonshire:
  Peterborough
Shropshire:
  Bridgenorth
  Great Wenlock
Somerset:
  Minehead
  Ilchester
  Milbournport
Southamptonshire:
  Petersfield
  Stockbridge
  Newtown
  Christchurch
  Whitchurch
  Lymington
Staffordshire:
  Stafford
  Tamworth
Suffolk:
  Aldborough
  Eye
Surrey:
  Southwark
  Bletchingley
  Ryegate

Gatton
Haselmere
Sussex:
  Horsham
  Midhurst
  Lewes
  New Shoreham
  Bramber
  Steyning
  East Grinstead
  Arundel
Wiltshire:
  Downton
  Hindon
  Westbury
  Heytesbury
  Ludgershall
  Great Bedwin
  Old Sarum
  Cricklade
Worcestershire:
  Droitwich
Yorkshire:
  Burrowbrig
  Knaresborough
  Malton
  Thirsk
  Aldborough
  Northallerton

SELECT BIBLIOGRAPHY

ANON., *Law of Corporations* (London, 1702).

BACON, M., *Abridgement of the Laws of England*, 7th edn. (Strahan, 1832).

BLACKSTONE, W., *Commentaries*, 4 vols. (1826 edn.).

BRADY, R., *Historical Treatise on Cities and Boroughs* (London, 1777).

BROOKE, R., *La Graunde Abridgement* (London, 1586).

BROWNING, A., 'Party Organisation in the Reign of Charles II', *Royal Hist. Soc. Trans.*, xxx (1948), 21.

(with D. J. Milne) 'An Exclusion Division List', *Bull. Inst. Hist. Res.*, xxiii (1950), 205.

BURNET, G., *History of My Own Time*, 6 vols., ed. Airy (Oxford, 1897).

CARDEN, P. T., 'Powers of Common Law Corporations', 26 *L.Q.R.* 320 (1910).

CLARKE, J. S., *Life of James II*, 2 vols. (London, 1916).

COKE, E., *Institutes*, 4 parts (Hargrave Edition, 1794).

COKE, R., *Detection of the Court and State etc.*, (1694).

CUNNINGHAM, T., *Historical Account of the Rights of Election etc.* (1783).

FEILING, K., *History of the Tory Party* (Oxford, 1950).

FOXCROFT, H. C., *Halifax* (Cambridge, 1946).

GEORGE, R. H., 'Parliamentary Elections and Electioneering in 1685', *Royal Hist. Soc. Trans.*, xix (1936), 167.

'Charters Granted to Parliamentary Corporations in 1688', *Eng. Hist. Rev.*, lv (1940), 47.

GLOVER, W., *Treaties on the Law of Municipal Corporations* (London, 1841).

GRANT, J., *Law of Corporations* (London, 1850).

GUILDHALL RECORD OFFICE, *Journals of the Common Council*.

Repertories of the Court of Aldermen.

HALLIS, F., *Corporate Personality* (Oxford, 1930).

HERBERT, W., *History of the Twelve Great Livery Companies of London* (London, 1887).

HISTORICAL MANUSCRIPTS COMMISSION, *Ormonde Papers* V and VI.

Twelfth Report.

Thirteenth Report.

HOLDSWORTH, SIR W. S., *History of English Law*, 16 vols. (London, 1966).

JAMES, A. T., *Municipal Corporations* (London, 1851).

'J.E.', *Charters of the City of London* (1693).

JONES, J. R., *The First Whigs* (Oxford, 1961).

'Shaftesbury's Worthy Men', *Bull. Inst. Hist. Res.*, xxx (1943/5), 232.

'James II's Whig Collaborators', *Historical Journal*, iii (1960), 65.

KELLET, J. R., *The Causes and Progress of the Financial Decline of the Corporation of London, 1660–1694* (Ph.D. Thesis, London, 1952).

KYD, S., *Law of Corporations*, 2 vols. (London, 1793–4).

LASKI, H. J.,'The Early History of Corporations in England', 30 *Harv. L. R.*, 561 (1916–17).

LONDON GAZETTE, Nos. 1835, 1837, 2388, 2390.

LUBASZ, N., 'The Corporate Borough in the Common Law of the Late Year Book Period', 80 *L.Q.R.* 228.

LUTTRELL, N., *A Brief Historical Relation of State Affairs 1678–1714*, 6 vols. (Oxford, 1857).

MACAULAY, BARON T. B., *History of England* (London, 1907).

MADOX, T., *Firma Burgi* (1726).

MAITLAND, F. W., *Introduction to Gierke: Genossenschaftsrecht* (Cambridge, 1900).

MAITLAND, W., *History of London*, 2 vols. (1756).

MAXWELL, J. S. and MAXWELL, L. F., *A Legal Bibliography of the British Commonwealth*, i and ii (London, 1957).

MEREWETHER, H. A., and STEPHENS, A. J., *History of the Boroughs and Municipal Corporations*, 3 vols. (London, 1853).

NORTH, R., *Lives of the Norths* (London, 1890).

NORTON, G., *Commentaries on the History of London* (London, 1869).

PAMPHLETS, *Case of the Charter of London Stated* (1683).
Defence of the Charter etc. of the City of London (1682).
The Forfeiture of London's Charter: An Impartial Account of the Several Seizures etc. (1682).
The Lord Mayor of London's Vindication (1682).
A Modest Inquiry Concerning the Election of Sheriffs of London etc. (1682).
The Pleadings, Arguments etc. on the Quo Warranto (1690).
The Privileges of the Citizens of London etc. (1682).

PAPILLON, A. F. W., *Memoirs of Thomas Papillon* (Reading, 1887).

POLLOCK, SIR F., 'Theory of Corporations in Common Law', 27 *L.Q.R.* 232.

POLLOCK, SIR F., and MAITLAND, F. W., *History of the Common Law*, 2 vols. (Cambridge, 2nd edn. 1898).

PORRIT, E., *The Unreformed House of Commons*, 2 vols. (Cambridge, 1903).

PULLING, A., *Treatise on the Laws and Customs of the City of London* (London, 1842).

RECORD COMMISSION, *Placita de Quo Warranto* (1818).

RERESBY, SIR J., *Memoirs*, ed. A. Browning (Jackson, 1936).

ROYAL COMMISSION ON MUNICIPAL CORPORATIONS, *Report* (1835).

SACRET, J. H., 'The Restoration Government and Municipal Corporations', *Eng. Hist. Rev.*, xlv (1930), 232.

SHARPE, R. R., *London and the Kingdom* (London, 1894).

SHEPPARD, W., *Of Corporations* (1659).

SMITH, H. A., *Law of Associations* (Oxford, 1914).

SMITH, J., *Select Cases on Private Corporations* (Cambridge, Mass., 1897).

SOMERS, LORD, *Tracts*, viii (1812).

STATE PAPERS, 1660–85, 1689–92.

STATE TRIALS, Cobbett Edition, 1810, viii.

SUTHERLAND, D., *Quo Warranto Proceedings in the Reign of Edward I* (Oxford, 1964).

VICTORIA COUNTY HISTORIES

WANG, K. C., *The Incorporate Person* (Ph.D. Thesis, London, 1942).

WEBB, S. and B., *English Local Government* (London, 1924).

INDEX